Physicians:
Money for Life

The physician's guide to retirement savings

"Rule No. 1: Never lose money.

Rule No. 2: Never forget rule No. 1."

—Warren Buffet

Dennis M. Postema

Second edition: March 2014

Praise for *Physicians: Money for Life*

"*Physicians: Money for Life* makes a powerful case for the indexed annuity. I admire how Dennis Postema takes a stand and supports it with passion, research and case studies. Dennis's position is so convincing that I will be sending a copy of his book to my financial advisor clients. If you are a physician and concerned at all about outliving your retirement funds, this a MUST read."

Sandy Schussel
Business Coach for Financial Advisors
Author of: *The High Diving Board* and *Become a Client Magnet*
http://sandyschussel.com

"As an insurance professional, I really enjoyed the easy reading and analogies. This is a book that every agent who works with physicians should read and they need to get copies for their clients. This is by far the best book I have ever seen that explains the Lifetime Guaranteed Income and insurance products that will make your clients or prospects wake up and realize that their stock broker will make them just that ... broker!"

Celeste duPreez
Senior Marketer
-bhcmarketing

"*Physicians: Money for Life* is a must-read book for a physician nearing or in retirement. It has clear, real-life examples on how to gain a handle on one's retirement income. If you are concerned about if you can retire or how your savings can last your retirement years, *Physicians: Money for Life* will open your eyes to what is possible.

In addition to the real-life examples, Mr. Postema also provides in-depth details on the 'how and why' of the topic. It is a book that reads easily for those who just want the basics and it provides deeper insight to those wanting the specifics.

In today's environment of low bank interest rates and a very volatile stock market, *Physicians: Money for Life* is a book that should be read by every physician age 60 years old and older."

Jerry Hraban, CLU, ChFC, RHU
Founder
Premier Insurance Partner, LLC
Author of *Extreme Producers: Their Insights and Secrets*

"Physicians: Money for Life was very well researched and extremely informative. I can relate to being at an age where retirement is not something off in the distance but right around the corner. Guaranteed income is a 'hot' topic and a very important one in a person's later years. Boomers/Seniors are bombarded with information and have a difficult time in determining the right path to take. Your book clearly outlines the challenges and solutions to the income dilemma. The book got me to see this topic in a different light. Thank you for sharing such thought-provoking and meaningful information."

Keith A. Hanson, CLU, ChFC, RHU

Vice President

Premier Insurance Partner, LLC

"Dennis M. Postema is a unique individual. As President of the National Association of Medicare Supplement Advisors, Inc., I got to know Dennis several years ago. Needless to say, our relationship has developed due to Dennis's ability to grasp and understand insurance matters far beyond my own abilities. In short, I have great respect for him.

He is determined to educate himself, his agents and his clients in a highly admirable fashion. His book, *Physicians: Money for Life*, is absolutely full of retirement and annuity hints that go far beyond normal insurance industry standards. He educates his clientele and readers of his books in a fashion that is an easy read, and in a way that the reader doesn't have to be the proverbial 'rocket scientist.'

In this volume, Dennis addresses several important retirement matters. No one before him has offered the advice he shares with you. Thousands of physicians have found out too late that there are steps they can take to ensure they do not run out of money during retirement.

Dennis solves these problems for you—ahead of time. Take heed."

Ron Iverson
President and Executive Director
National Association of Medicare Supplement Advisors, Inc.

Table of Contents

About the Author

Dennis M. Postema, RFC, is a successful entrepreneur, best-selling author, coach, speaker and registered financial consultant. He is the founder of MotivationandSuccess.com, StoriesofPerseverance.org, FinancingYourLife.com and TheRetirementInstitute.org.

Over the past 12 years, Dennis has taught clients, agents and associates how to find motivation and ascend psychological barriers to achieve success. His dedication to improving lives has led him to work with renowned motivational and self-help industry heavyweights such as Jack Canfield and Brian Tracy.

Dennis' personal experience with tragedy, life-changing surgeries and health issues has given him a unique perspective on what it means to achieve success and what's really standing in the way of it. He channels that perspective into educational and motivational books and programs in the topics of finance, perseverance, success and business.

His focus on helping clients, rather than simply selling products, landed him on the cover of *Agents Sales Journal*

(*Senior Market Edition*) in 2011. In 2012, he was a recipient of the 10 Under 40 Award given by the Defiance Chamber of Commerce. He was also awarded the 2013 Distinguished Alumni Award from his alma mater, Northwest State Community College, for his success in the industry and community. His contribution to Jack Canfield's book, *Dare to Succeed*, earned him an Editor's Choice award.

Dedication

To my better half, my wife Jen—you're my best friend and full support system. Thank you for putting up with me during all of my projects that make our schedules crazy.

To my family, friends and team who make all that I do possible.

Finally, to all those people out there either retired or soon to be retiring, it's my hope that this will help give you unbiased advice that can truly educate you to make the decisions that will help you succeed in the golden years.

Disclaimer

All information provided in this book has been researched and is accurate and complete to the best of the author's knowledge. The author is not responsible for any errors or omissions and there is no guarantee of completeness, accuracy or timeliness regarding the information provided throughout this book. You may use this information however you feel necessary, but you assume full responsibility for any potential loss that may occur from the use of this information.

Dennis M. Postema will not be liable for any direct, indirect, consequential, special, incidental or punitive damages or any other damages whatsoever. Under no circumstance will Dennis M. Postema, related partnerships, corporations or other direct relationships of the author be held liable to you or anyone else for any information relied upon by you from this book. You assume full risk and responsibility for how you use the information provided in this book.

All information in this book that was accurate at the time of publication may change at any time. Changes in the market, laws or other circumstances that arise may cause these facts to change and the information provided throughout this book may not be assumed to be correct at all times. Individual environmental changes can cause the results in this book to vary at any time. All decisions made due to information provided in this book are the sole responsibility of the reader.

Foreword

During the 40 years I spent in the insurance business, I always devoted a substantial amount of time to educating the public about insurance, its many uses and its variety of coverage options. I spent even more time helping solve the specialty retirement saving needs of a very important group of professionals in our society: physicians. What I should have done was put my information into a book like Dennis Postema has done here.

Many physicians and other health professionals don't realize just how amazing and versatile insurance products, including annuities, can be and how well-suited they are to ensuring a timely retirement. Without any idea of what the insurance world has to offer, these individuals don't know what questions to ask their agents or what to expect—or demand—out of a properly designed policy or contract. *Physicians: Money for Life* can change all that.

The book is detailed, easy to read and gives retirees and those closing in on their retirement years a fantastic basis for designing their future and controlling their income. The chapter *Better Retirement Planning with Annuities* goes into such detail about annuities, riders and payout options that anyone reading it will be able to quickly grasp the topics and more easily determine what direction they should take when designing their retirement future.

Dennis has outlined a great deal of information in a simple but effective way that truly educates the reader. Anyone considering putting money into an annuity will be able to do so with full confidence in what they are getting into.

I would recommend that medical professionals with a sincere desire to retire early consider what Dennis has to say. I have found this book enormously educational—and I think you will too.

Ken Varga
CEO
http://kenvarga.com

A graduate of Rutgers University, Ken Varga has spent his career as a business owner, consultant, lecturer, author and highly acclaimed speaker.

Author's Note

The purpose of this book is simple:

I want to help physicians.

I want to make high-income individuals in the medical community, those people who dedicate their lives to healing the sick, aware of the opportunities that exist for a safe, comfortable retirement—opportunities they might know nothing about.

As a professional in the retirement account industry, I can tell you there is one question that almost every retiree asks, no matter what his or her preretirement income was. That question is: "What if I run out of money?" The purpose of this book is to address that question by showing you how to make your savings grow for retirement and last a lifetime.

Now, I have seen how the dilemma of running out of retirement money affects my friends, family and complete strangers, and the recurring issue that comes up is people are tired of their CDs in the bank not paying enough interest to keep up with inflation and the rising cost of medical expenses. If they didn't play it safe by putting their money in CDs, they were losing money over and over again in the market. These individuals are the ones who keep hearing, "Oh, the losses are all on paper, the market is going to come back," or, "You don't lose until you sell," or, "Just wait it out."

But the reality is that physicians like you just don't have the time to "wait it out" and, with your already hectic schedule, you don't have the wherewithal to keep a constant watch on the market. You spend your whole life working toward retirement and you deserve to enjoy those years without having to worry about outliving your income. That's why I offer you the same advice I offer my friends and family— advice on making it through retirement without worry thanks to a low-risk investment that keeps up with inflation and ensures that you never run out of money. The purpose of this book is to show you how to do that.

As a physician, you know the value of hunches, but you also know the value of facts. Investing on hunches alone is dangerous, just as treating a patient or performing surgery on a hunch can be risky. That's why I try to give you as many facts as possible in this book so you can make an informed decision on how to put a plan in force with an advisor who will help you save your retirement money *and* ensure that outliving your income is not an option.

Introduction

Retirement planning seems basic and perhaps at its core, it is. Most individuals think of retirement planning as a three-step process:

1. Save money.

2. Earn interest.

3. Retire with a reduced budget.

But if your retirement plan consists of nothing more sophisticated than those elements, you are oversimplifying it in a very dangerous way. It's almost like taking the mantra "an apple a day keeps the doctor away" as a literal prescription for lifelong good health. When you oversimplify retirement planning, you will find that you are unprepared for many of the financial challenges retirees face, such as:

- Outliving your savings

- High tax burdens

- Inflation

- Increasing medical expenses

- Market risk

While each of the individual concerns on that list is a problem worthy of a book on its own, I find that they all add up to one giant problem—something actuaries like to refer to as *longevity risk*.

There is probably not much you want more than to live a long, healthy life after retiring from the working world, but a long life is also a burden to a retiree who is trying to live only on the money he managed to set aside before retirement. With no new, dependable source of income, retirees face fear every day: the fear that they will outlive what's in their IRA, 401(k) and pension; the fear that Social Security won't be there to help back them up and pay what they're owed; the fear that rising prices on everyday staples will drain their savings more quickly than they expected.

This problem especially concerns high-income pre- and postretirees. For these individuals, the cards are mostly dealt. It's not as if they have decades upon decades of working years ahead of them to correct for any lackluster returns or halfhearted saving attempts during their youth and, after working hard to acquire a certain standard of living over the years, they're not likely to want to lower their standards after retiring. Additionally, they must still contend with a lengthening life span—with medical innovation and healthier standards of living, experts suggest that longevity is becoming more commonplace, and more of a risk to retirement accounts.

This creates a weird tipping point for preretirees who may not have realized that the odds of living well into their 90s would be so high. They may instead have based their retirement savings goals and plans on life expectancy charts from 20 years ago—charts that are sorely inaccurate. Here's a great example of how out of touch those charts were, a fact you likely noticed in your medical practice. In 1990 the Centers for Disease Control life expectancy table anticipated that the average male between ages 40-45 would live to about age 75-80. Eighteen years later, in 2008, those same individuals were between 58 and 63, and their new life expectancy range was between ages 80.5 to 82.5. In 2013, 50 percent of individuals who are 65 can expect to live to age 92. Life keeps extending—retirement savings, however, do not.

Another aspect working against retirees in terms of their longevity risk is inflation and taxes, which are weirdly proportionate to longevity. The older you get, the more likely inflation will have increased your expenses and the more likely tax rates will have gone up, something that can be especially damaging to physicians who want a stable, above-average income into retirement.

Today, I want to give you some financial power over your longevity. I want you to look forward to seeing your 92-year-old face in the mirror and not dread the thought of having to skip that vacation in favor of maintaining a more practical budget.

Here, I'll show you the simple, flexible, affordable way to combat all of your postretirement financial concerns while turning your retirement savings into a dependable, *guaranteed* income that provides a consistent, meaningful postretirement benefit able to help you control tax liabilities, limit risks, accommodate inflation and pay for expenses, all while making sure you don't outlive your retirement savings.

Chapter 1

The Economic Problems Facing Today's Preretirees

According to the Pew Research Center, around 10,000 baby boomers turn 65 each day and will continue to do so for the next 17 years. Because 65 is the traditional retirement age, and there are roughly 76 million people currently on the verge of retirement, that makes retirement planning a significant concern for a large percentage of our population.

It's an extremely scary time to be retiring as a member of the upper middle class. In 2008 Ernst & Young released its report titled "Retirement Vulnerability of New Retirees: The Likelihood of Outliving Their Financial Assets."[1] The report noted that three out of five retirees could expect to outlive their savings without doing anything fancy or unusually risky but by simply trying to maintain their preretirement standard of living after they'd retired. The report goes on to discuss the undeniable fact that retirees should be prepared to reduce their standard of living by approximately 32 percent, primarily because of fluctuating returns on investments and continually lengthening life expectancies leaving them with more years—sometimes decades—for their retirement fund to support them through. Add to this the increasing medical costs faced by the aging population and you have a recipe for financial disaster.

However, even more startling was the report's finding that individuals who were seven years out from retirement at the time of the study would actually have to reduce their standard of living by *45 percent* in order to avoid running out of retirement resources, unless they found the means of creating a guaranteed, lifetime income after retirement.

Doctors, generally considered high-income earners, are not exempt from these concerns. In fact, in a 2012 survey the Physicians Foundation found that 60 percent of respondents would retire immediately—if they only had the means to do so. It's possible that, if some of these respondents were willing to reduce their standard of living substantially—like by the 32 or 45 percent numbers above—they could eek out enough income from their present savings. My answer to that line of thinking is why should they have to?

Once there was a time when an employer-sponsored defined benefit plan would have provided that guaranteed income stream. But over the past few decades, these plans have mostly been phased out in favor of less expensive, less risky plans such as 401(k)s, which place the burden of generating retirement security solely on the participating employees. Unfortunately for physicians, these plans also place limits on what can be contributed and who can contribute to those levels. In 2013 the maximum salary deferral for a 401(k) is $17,500 with a $5,500 catch-up contribution for those aged 50 and up. When adding on the employer's match, the total allowable is $51,000. That may seem like enough if you start saving at age 30, but as the American Academy of Orthopaedic Surgeons recently reported, most orthopaedic surgeons don't start saving for retirement until they reach age 50, giving them very few years to save enough, especially with such harsh contribution limits. This is not surprising when you consider the bills that new doctors starting their careers face as they try to establish their practice and their name within their specialty. One must also consider that the starting salary of many specialties, according to the 2011-2012 Physician Salary Survey conducted by Profiles, is much lower than the national six-year practicing average, which puts them at an additional disadvantage for retirement savings. At six years into their careers, many doctors are finally feeling stable and may be trying to start a family—a difficult time to expect an individual to adjust his or her lifestyle and start setting aside $40,000 or more per year.

Of course, it's not just a lifestyle adjustment that needs to occur; preretirees in all professions must also become sophisticated investors overnight so they can make the right decisions to allow their savings to grow into sufficient sources of support through a long retirement. The stock market is not a kind place for dabblers and the inexperienced, and those risks that employers want to avoid are now squarely on the shoulders of employees who may never have traded stocks before in their entire lives.

Physicians go to medical school for many years. Between school, labs and residency, they immerse themselves in their specialties. They take these years and all this time immersing themselves because that's what it takes to become an expert medical practitioner.

Just as one wouldn't expect an individual who'd once read a physiology book to perform brain surgery, neither should anyone expect an individual who's read a book on investing to have the same skill as a financial planner. Consider all the giant financial shifts we've had over the past two decades that even some of the savviest financial advisors didn't see coming. The first market meltdown during this period occurred in the early 2000s when the tech stock bubble burst. Technology stocks, the new darlings of experienced investors and novices alike in the late '90s, were bolstered by venture capital, but few made a profit in the years that followed. Then came the antitrust case with Microsoft, pushing many investors out of love with tech stocks and creating a massive sale that gutted the sector and burst the bubble. After the tech bubble came 9/11, a time marked with global financial downturns, high insurance claims and fear—lots of fear about the vulnerability of our financial system. Between the popping tech bubble and 9/11, the S&P 500 lost 41 percent between 2000 and 2003. By 2007 we'd mostly recovered, but hovering above our heads was a real estate bubble ready to burst, which it finally did in 2008— the fallout of which has continued for years.

Even worse, 401(k) plans saw average losses of 25 to 30 percent—some losses experienced by people with enough time to gain that money back, and some experienced by those who didn't.

At its lowest point, the Dow Jones Industrial Average had fallen by roughly 53 percent in seventeen months.*

Like a starfish repeatedly growing back its limbs, our financial system has once again rebounded, only to face dips upon worries surrounding Europe's spiraling debt crisis, concerns that the fiscal cliff would be our financial demise, and that the national debt will hit its ceiling on February 15, bringing about crippling budget restrictions.

*The Dow Jones hit 14,093 during the week of 10/08/07 and 6,626.94 the week of 3/02/09.

In 2010, the general feeling of fear and apprehension got a little more real for pre- and postretirees, whether they realized it or not. In that year, Social Security payouts exceeded Social Security taxes collected for the first time in 27 years.

And now we've made it to the apex of the terrible place we've reached. Because we know that the stock market is a sophisticated, unreliable bedfellow, and we know that retirees—more than anything—want to secure a lifetime income. In fact, a study by insurance giant Allianz showed that almost twice as many people feared outliving their retirement savings as feared death itself.

My goal, however, is not to give you a set of problems without solutions. It's to help you understand what could be working against your ability to provide a comfortable, secure future for yourself after retirement and to find a solution for it—a solution that may just be found in annuities.

I also want you to reconsider some of your preconceptions. While I understand the power of annuities to provide a safe, secure, reliable retirement income, more than 50 percent of consumers polled by Allianz had a negative view of annuities, a view that had been formed anywhere from 10 to 20 years ago.

I hope that you can push aside any bias you have for annuities, that you can see the man behind the curtain and recognize that the moving parts of an annuity are transparent, trustworthy and offer you one of the best chances of securing money for life.

Chapter 2

Redefining Financial Planning Rules

During a bull market—that exciting time when the market goes up and people think the upswing will continue indefinitely—investors tend to focus on making financial decisions that will help them grow their savings. They focus on earning and accumulating more. More, more, and then some more. But a financial advisor is not necessarily supposed to support that mindset. Often considered the creator of the field of financial planning, Loren Dutton, founder of the College for Financial Planning, defined the purpose of a financial planner or advisor as:

"Helping average people learn how to spend, save, invest, insure and plan wisely for the future, to achieve financial independence."

Looking at the history of the stock market, we consistently see periods of boom followed by periods of bust. The down market periods drain some of the earnings taken during the bull markets and they generally last more than a decade. While some individuals may get through the down period and have time to recover their losses when the market improves, if you are within a decade of retiring or already retired when the cyclical downturn arrives—and believe me, it will arrive—your savings can be irretrievably gutted.

Instead, it's better for the modern pre- and postretiree to focus on preservation rather than chasing returns. Nothing in life is guaranteed, and even less is guaranteed in the world of investing. But the one thing any pre- and postretiree can rely on is the pile of funds they saved out of their salary. While savers want those dollars to grow and thrive, an individual's top priority should be in maintaining the stronghold they have over their savings—not letting a single, solitary penny of those hard-earned funds go to waste.

For example, consider the individual who invests in interest-earning, FDIC-insured CDs. That individual may not see his account value grow exponentially, but he does see it remain stable and earn a steady, guaranteed interest payment. He is, therefore, preserving his retirement without hiding his cash under the mattress. An annuity offers an even safer, more predictable stream of income along with an even more secure method of capital preservation and better opportunity for growth.

Sadly, not every investor or every advisor recognizes the true value of preservation, and that can result in incomprehensible loss. Not just of money, but of dreams, security and comfort.

Let's meet Steven and Deborah. Steven spent his entire childhood dreaming of being a physician of some kind. In medical school, he finally found his calling: cardiology. During his residency, he met Deborah on one of his few nights off. Theirs was a whirlwind romance, with marriage just a few months after his residency was completed. Deborah had career aspirations of her own, so not only did she care for their two children but she was also a teacher for many years.

Steven and Deborah had many goals for their retirement savings. Ultimately, they tried to save as much as they could each year in order to help secure a comfortable retirement. They planned to spend this time visiting their grandchildren, traveling to some of the more far-flung corners of the world they hadn't yet explored, and spending lots of time relaxing together.

The first thing they each did with every paycheck was to make a contribution to their various savings accounts. In fact, they both automated their contributions so that they were paid out before their bills.

In 2001 and 2002, like many other investors, they went through a rough patch. At the worst point, their accounts lost 28 percent of their gains and principal, partially due to some tech investments and partially due to 9/11. By 2007, they had more than regained their losses and were finally feeling secure again.

In October 2007, the Dow hit what was, at the time, its highest point—14,164. Because Steven and Deborah's accounts were benefiting from this rise, they felt ready to start planning their retirement. They decided that Deborah, who was 62, would retire first. After she did, they'd move the $600,000 balance of her 403(b) to the same, big-named firm that had Steven's 401(k).

Steven wanted to stay in his practice until age 65, for the benefit of his partners, which gave him another year to work and save. At the time, Steven's 401(k) balance was $3,000,000 and all of their outstanding debts were paid.

On September 15, 2008, Steven turned 65 and his practice threw him a touching retirement party. The last thing he did before leaving the office that day was log into both his and Deborah's accounts to verify their balances, which were still holding a combined total of roughly $3,600,000.

They spent the first week and a half on a cruise. It was a short trip, but an important event to mark the transition of the couple into retirement. What Deborah and Steven didn't realize was that, while they were watching the whales off the coast of Alaska, their account balances were dropping by 10 percent during one short trading day as panic set in over the housing market.

When they arrived home and heard the news, Steven logged into their accounts and saw the dramatic drop in value. He called their broker, but the man had no sense of urgency whatsoever. He told Steven that the losses on a single day were not real and would certainly not remain over the long haul. He also told Steven that as long as he didn't sell and realize the losses, they weren't anything to consider.

Steven remembered the patients he'd had over the last decade of his career who'd run to the Internet and diagnosed themselves. When Steven would tell them that their "diagnosis" wasn't correct, they often had this look in their eyes as if they didn't quite believe the cardiologist with decades of education and experience. Steven knew that sometimes, you just have to trust the professionals, and that's what he did. For the next few weeks he made it a point to ignore the television news and the Internet news sites and went back to enjoying retirement. Somehow along the way, he even managed to forget about the losses and enjoyed his new freedom. On October 22, when his and Deborah's account statements arrived, he hadn't braced himself to see the additional 20 percent loss on both of their accounts—on top of the 10 percent they'd lost weeks before.

Once again, he called his broker, and once again, his broker said it was nothing but a paper loss, and Steven put the losses, and the market, out of his mind.

He and Deborah took a road trip to the Grand Canyon, which they'd somehow both never seen. When they returned and picked up their mail from the post office, Steven found the November account statements for him and Deborah. Ripping open the envelope, he was actually optimistic that he would see how right his broker had been. But when he unfolded the paper inside and saw the numbers printed on it, he was momentarily confused, thinking maybe the brokerage had made a mistake and sent him the wrong person's statement. Because while he'd believed his broker that there was nothing to worry about, the $3,000,000 401(k) balance had fallen more than 50 percent to $1,500,000. Steven and Deborah had lost over 51 percent of their money. Real money, paper money—life-sustaining money—in just over two months, the only months Steven had even spent as a retired person.

Deborah's account wasn't spared, either. It had fallen from $600,000 to $321,000, a 46.5 percent drop. Now Steven was going to have to consider washing his white coat and going back to the office.

It would be sad enough if this were a story unique to Steven and Deborah. In fact, it's a tragic fact that this same story has been repeated in household after household, and will continue to happen as the market exercises its cyclical nature for decades to come unless you do something to stop it. Unless you stop the sweeping tides of gains and losses and instead find a way to preserve your savings while creating a lifetime of stable, reliable income for yourself and your spouse.

It's devastating to think about how many preretirees and retirees who were in the market in 2008 saw their entire financial futures wiped out in one fell swoop. Depending on what happens in the economy and market and how long you live with risky investments and no undercurrent of safety, your retirement savings could be cut in half just like Steven and Deborah's—unless you make that change we hinted about above.

It's up to you to make sure that you are educated on what to do to make sure Steven and Deborah's story doesn't become yours, so you can sit back and enjoy retirement and never have to open a statement and feel the panic in the pit of your stomach as Steven did just two short months after his retirement.

Accumulation versus Preservation

When you are first beginning to save for retirement, and during the decades that follow, the importance of accumulation will have been, and continue to be, pounded into your head. When you begin to discuss preretirement or retirement with your broker, you may have had more discussion of accumulation, a concept that requires you to stay at least partially invested in risky stocks so that you can grow your money to support you during your entire retirement.

I do not want to downplay the importance of accumulation. Accumulation is still—and will always be—a vital part of saving for anything, especially retirement. But it's just that— one single part of your overall retirement plan. For physicians who want to create a high-income postretirement lifestyle but must do so around the constraints of aggressive retirement account contribution limits, the accumulation mindset can push you into riskier and riskier positions as you try to make up for contribution limits with growth—a very dangerous proposition. The days during which the market moved nowhere but up and accumulation was all we had to worry about are well over. In fact, they never really existed at all. The market has always gone through roller coaster periods of good and bad.

Accepting the Changing Waters

I want to teach you how to avoid that roller coaster without sacrificing your goals or comfort after retirement. Here's the thing that many brokers and advisors ignore: the financial planning waters have changed. Conservative wisdom and conventional methods will only take you so far. They are as ill-suited to the current market as trying to buy groceries with Confederate dollars.

When you get to the stage in life when retirement is about 10 to 15 years away, you need to switch your mindset out of the Accumulation Phase and into what I like to call the *Preservation and Distribution* phase; whether your money is in risky stocks, bonds or mutual funds, it can be lost to the whims of the investor-perception-driven market. And no one should risk her retirement to that.

Let's say that you need to go grocery shopping. You have a long list of items to buy and although you have what you think is enough cash to pay for everything on said list, you aren't sure—and you'd love to have a little extra. Would you stop off at the local gas station and use all of your grocery money to buy scratch-off tickets? But why not? After all, you could win enough to double or triple your grocery money! You know as well as I do that the chances of that are next to nothing and are certainly not worth the hefty risks involved. You already understand why it's not a good idea to invest in the stock market as you approach retirement—even if that's what all the stock jockeys are telling you to do.

Instead of focusing on what *not* to do when you're 10 to 15 years out from retirement, I like to stress to my clients that they focus on what their goals are for their retirement money, and I would suggest the same to you. By defining your goals, you will get to the root of where you do and do not want to put your money.

Points of Consideration

- Are you okay with risking everything in order to have the potential for a higher return? By risking it all, I do mean that you could lose everything you worked so hard to save.

- Do you have enough in CDs and other fixed investments that, if they continue to have low returns that don't keep up with inflation, you will not run out of money? There are many online calculators that can help you see what your low-interest, fixed accounts will grow to over time.

- Compare your "I told you so" points. Have you ever been stuck in that one lane of traffic that doesn't move? Then, as soon as there's an opening, you merge to the moving lane while your passenger says you shouldn't because the lane you're in is about to move. Then, just like clockwork, as soon as you're out of it—the lane you left starts moving and the new lane stops. This happens in many places, such as the supermarket checkout and the stock market.

Continued …

Ask yourself how you will feel if you put all your money into the market and lose 50 percent. Then, ask yourself how you'd feel if you put it into something more secure and made only 8 percent when the market has risen 10 percent. Which one hurts worse? Which situation is going to make that bitter "I told you so!" come out?

- What is most important to you at this phase of your life? Accumulating more dollars, or preserving what you've saved? Remember that the closer you are to retirement, the fewer working and earning years you have left. That leaves little time to regain what's been lost once it's gone.

- How much does control mean to you? Is it more important for you to be able to choose each individual investment you have, or is it more important to find a means of guaranteeing a postretirement income? Is it more important to trade individual positions and be exposed to market risks, or to find a safety net from the risk that also provides the means to lock in gains?

Moving from Accumulation to Preservation

Anyone who's reached their 50s or 60s truly needs to switch their mindset from accumulation to the preservation and income planning/distribution phase. The longevity of their comfortable retirement relies on it.

Things to think about in this phase include:

- **Market turbulence**

   I called it a roller coaster—because it is. But this roller coaster isn't just about a Sunday afternoon of fun with the grandkids—it's about life and death. It's about the sustainability of your lifestyle. It makes no sense to ride this roller coaster if there's another option.

- **Increase in the cost of living**

   Inflation is real, and not entirely comfortable. The rate of inflation for 2012 was 1.7 percent,[2] which means the cost of all goods and services in general rose by almost 2 percent. In the next 10 or 15 years, how much will these seemingly incremental changes collectively take out of your retirement savings?

Between 1999 and 2008, the Consumer Price Index increased roughly 29 percent.[3] That's a nightmare-inducing fact. And how much will other increases—those not due to regular inflation, but by other factors, such as depletion, environmental issues, regulatory changes, etc.—affect the power of your retirement dollars?

While some may try to convince you that investing in stocks is the only way to beat inflation, that simply isn't true. As you'll see in the next chapter, as many as 39 percent of publicly traded stocks have negative returns over the course of their lifetime. Add to this the general unpredictability of the stock market and the impossibility of isolating only the right stocks—those that will grow in value—in your portfolio, and you can see why little faith should be placed in the stock market when it comes to guaranteeing anything, much less a supplement for inflation.

Social Security generally does a cost-of-living adjustment (COLA), but with other costs rising unrelated to inflation, such as medical expenses, it's still going to come up short when retirees look at their year-to-year budgets.

- **Increased life expectancy**

It's nice that medical technology is sophisticated enough to offer us a longer life, but it's also expensive. Premiums for employer-sponsored health insurance rose 119 percent between 1999 and 2008.[4] And Medicare, as you probably know, isn't a magical panacea. Couples retired in 2012 are expected to pay $240,000 for postretirement healthcare expenses even with the help of Medicare.[5] And the later you retire, the higher that number will rise.

- **Social Security and other disappearing or less dependable sources of income**

According to the Social Security Administration, the trust fund in which they keep withheld taxes for payment of benefits will be empty by 2041. At that time, they expect to be able to collect taxes from workers for 78 percent[6] of the funds they are obligated to pay out. Where will they get the other 22 percent? Will they get it, or will Social Security payments fall short? Will the trust fund even hold out until 2041, or will it be depleted sooner? It's impossible to answer any of these questions with any authority. Either way, the Social Security withholding on a physician's income is very small—taxing only the first $113,700 as of 2013. That means the subsequent payment is not something you can rely on to replace much of your former, working income.

At the end of the day, you need to ask yourself a single, very important question: Is this going to get better or worse?

Chapter 3

Wall Street's Dirty Truth

My father-in-law called it a business decision. He said, "Choosing an index annuity over the stock market is truly a business decision. After all, could an advisor beat an index annuity over the next five years? It's possible, but highly unlikely over the long term. The best brokers and day traders out there are only right, at best, about 40 percent of the time."

If you're wondering why my father-in-law—a businessman who'd never sold insurance in his life—knew more than many Wall Street-focused advisors, the truth is that he didn't—he just said aloud what they wouldn't.

The Reality of Returns

In 2008, BlackStar Funds conducted a study[7] on the returns of the stocks on the Russell 3000, an index that represents 98 percent of all the public stocks out there. What they found in the performance of these stocks between 1983 and 2006 is worse than disturbing—it's downright distressing.

- Thirty-nine (39) percent of all the stocks in the index had a negative return over the stocks' lifetime.

- Sixty-four (64) percent underperformed the index itself (meaning that a small number of high-performing stocks were carrying the entire lot of them).

- Almost 20 percent of the stocks lost at least 75 percent of their value between 1983 and 2006.

- Just 10 percent of the stocks on the index were high performers, making returns of over 500 percent.

What do you think your chances—or any investor's chances for that matter—are of finding and investing in the right stocks? The ones that avoid being in the 64 percent that underperform the index, avoid being in the 39 percent that have negative returns, and avoid becoming one of the almost 20 percent that are just about worthless over time?

The truth is, it's a numbers game, which means most investors are more than likely to pick the wrong stocks and lose money. But why has Wall Street been completely mum about these findings? Why do they still refer to brokers who help hasten the downfall of our economy as "talent" deserving of great big bonuses, even as the financial walls are crashing down around us? For one simple reason: Wall Street makes money when investors invest.

Brokerage houses make a living on commissions, and commissions only occur when investors are buying and selling stocks. These days, as advisors more and more often suggest their clients move in and out of various positions in a futile effort to time the market, commissions are increasing and making the brokerages even more money than in decades past. In fact, in 2010, with just 7,500 companies, the total profits for the U.S. securities brokerage industry were $150 billion—and just 50 companies made 80 percent of that profit.[8]

Index annuities, on the other hand, have lower profit margins than mutual funds with their excessive management fees and stocks with giant commissions. They even have a lower profit margin for the insurer than most variable annuities.

But what about advisors? Why aren't advisors giving their clients the inside track to this more secure method of creating a retirement income? Unfortunately, the answer to this question is easy: index annuities offer agents a one-time commission. Stock and mutual fund trades make money each time they're executed. Can you imagine the career of a doctor or surgeon who had only a 10 percent success rate on a relatively simple procedure or in treating a particular illness? Your patients would never put up with such a low chance of recovery when there are better options out there, so why should investors?

If you talk to twenty advisors, you'll get twenty opinions about what you should and shouldn't invest in, or where the safest place for your retirement savings is. I firmly believe that if you want to risk some of your portfolio, that's fine—but as far as I'm concerned retirement accounts should be off-limits to risk. There is no reason with an index annuity (which some consider a hybrid annuity) to risk actual retirement accounts. Traditional brokers do not want you to know about these products—period. I like to err on the side of safety to be able to sleep at night.

Now, if you have an advisor who is doing a great job and believes differently than I do, it may mean he is a good fit for you and the decisions you make together about managing your portfolio are appropriate for your situation and goals. I developed my investing and saving philosophies by watching the roller coaster of the market over the past decade. Combine that with the many years I've spent in the industry and the countless hours I've dedicated toward studying it, and the result is someone who advises clients to be ultraconservative when dealing with their retirement nest eggs.

I might change my tune if the world were a different place. If you could participate in the very intriguing market gains with no chance of losses. If the economy were different. If inflation and regulation weren't such catalysts for negative financial changes. If my "ifs" became realities, I would say, "Sign me up," any day of the week. But until that day—a day I strongly suspect will never come—I think it's not worth it to get greedy over all the hype and drink the Kool-Aid in exchange for such a small spread of what the market *could* do.

Straightening Out the Bell Curve

Many advisors promote the concept of stock returns always, over time, growing. They support this theory by showing investors a statistical illustration of growth over time, called a bell curve because it is shaped like a bell.

They insist that this illustration of long-term growth means that all stocks will generally follow a predictable outcome over the long haul and few will deviate from that expected outcome or, in the case of finance, return.

For years now, brokers and advisors have spread the myth that dollar-cost averaging, a method of making regular, periodic purchases of stock so that you can take advantage of the low prices to offset the high prices in this roller coaster market, is a great idea for investors, Many believe that's it's especially good for physician investors with busy practices who don't have time to watch the market and can't exactly stop in the middle of surgery or an exam to start selling or buying positions that seem to be in flux.

Further, these advisors say that collectively, over time, stock portfolios do nothing but grow in value, as is illustrated by their sample of a bell curve. Their mantra about the bell shape of returns—small at the beginning, then blossoming out a few years later—is repeated so often, it has reached legend status and is still believed, even though it's been shown to be false.

Without a doubt, you can look at select periods and see where the bell curve return is accurate. But what is being measured? An index, like the Russell Index discussed above, in which the majority of stocks represented are losing money and just a chosen few are pulling up the ranks? What about the select period of time being analyzed? Is it a period that includes a market implosion such as the one we had between 2007 and 2009? It sure doesn't seem like someone retiring during those years would have caught the big end of the bell. How likely is it that your returns will happen to fall into such a period of good luck and blossom out into the bell shape? It may, if you buy into the index itself, as you can through an indexed annuity's Russell subaccount, but with individual stocks, it's doubtful you'll pick the right ones.

What has actually been found is that market returns are generally skewed to be extremely positive or extremely negative,[9] and few follow the guaranteed, gradual growth presented by Wall Street.

But enough with the *ifs* and *coulds*. Let's look at some cold, hard facts and explore annuity performance against that of the stock market. It's important to note that in the graph on the following page, I am using numbers from a Wharton Financial Institution study conducted in 2010. Why is this important? Well, first, you shouldn't take someone else's word about the power of any investment. Instead, you should look at facts—such as this study. The reason this study is so powerful is that they reviewed actual annuity contracts that were sold and recorded interest that was really credited to the contract holders. That means that these numbers aren't a best-case scenario or a worst-case scenario—they are true and factual based on real events.

The study also notes that not only have annuity returns historically been competitive with stock and bond portfolios, but also they were designed to have limited downside risk and healthy returns in up markets.

Another interesting point made within this report is that it notes something about studies that have criticized fixed-index annuities. The report discusses how these critical pieces often utilize hypothetical data—something that can be easily manipulated in order to make one investment appear more worthy than another. That's just another reason that cold, hard facts are your friend when measuring various investment options and risks.

Okay—onto the numbers. This graph from the Wharton study compares the average returns of the S&P 500 with the average returns of fixed-index annuities from 1997 to 2010.

In the far left column you can see the time period of the comparison.

Period	S&P 500 Index Return	FIA Average Return	Number of FIAs	Return Range
1997-2002	9.39%	9.19%	5	7.80% to 12.16%
1998-2003	-0.42%	5.46%	13	3.00% to 7.97%
1999-2004	-2.77%	4.69%	8	3.00% to 6.63%
2000-2005	-3.08%	4.33%	28	0.85% to 8.66%
2001-2006	5.11%	4.36%	13	1.91% to 6.55%
2002-2007	13.37%	6.12%	23	3.00% to 8.39%
2003-2008	3.18%	6.05%	19	3.00% to 7.80%
2004-2009	-1.05%	4.19%	27	2.25% to 6.83%
2005-2010	-1.47%	3.89%	36	2.33% to 7.10%

Chart and disclaimer courtesy of Wharton Financial Institutions Center Personal Finance, Real World Index Annuity Returns, December 2010.[9] Note: All returns shown above are annualized (geometric) rates of return. The S&P index returns are not meant to proxy for index mutual fund returns, which would include dividends, expense ratios (the least costly have featured approximately 20 b.p. per year), trading costs (another 30 b.p. per year), tracking error and taxes. Rather, they are to reference what happened to the most popular index to which many FIAs are linked through some formula. Later, we consider total returns (including dividends, but not expenses and trading costs) on the S&P 500 stocks.

Sometimes, it's not about investing in an ideal world—or finding the ideal investments in a less-than-ideal world. It's about looking at the facts and comparing options. It's about doing our own research and coming up with reasonable financial solutions that benefit us more than Wall Street, advisors, brokers and so on.

Finding Solutions

In the last chapter, we talked about the unfortunate situation that retirees Steven and Deborah faced just months after leaving the working world behind.

Their story is not unique, and it's not the only story out there. Some of the stories I can share seem as though they will end with similar tragic results, but because the individuals involved finally took advice from a knowledgeable advisor, they achieved happier endings than you'd expect.

Through the next few chapters, let's follow along with another couple, James and Sharon, and see how they managed to cure their retirement funding and legacy planning issues very simply with an indexed annuity and a guaranteed minimum income benefit rider. At the end of each chapter, we'll talk about how the concerns in that chapter affected James and Sharon and other clients, and we'll discuss how they resolved them.

The Story of James and Sharon

James and Sharon are a married couple in their 60s. In 1973, James finished his residency and began working as an ER doctor. He remained at the same hospital for 35 years and retired in 2008 at age 63.

Sharon was a housewife until their first child was born. Then she was a stay-at-home mother. They had two more children, giving Sharon a rambunctious, close-knit family for whom to care.

As a stay-at-home mother, Sharon has no retirement savings and has not paid into the Social Security system. That means James' retirement savings and meager Social Security payout must support both of them during retirement. Whatever is left of their savings after they've gone will create the basis of the legacy they leave to their children and any grandchildren.

Chapter 4

Retirement Planning Challenges

We work our whole lives with a single mantra playing through our heads: "Save for retirement." We budget carefully and learn about our employer's vesting and contribution matching policies; we consider our self-employed retirement plan options;

"With all the uncertainty facing retirees, it's no wonder that their number-one fear is that they will outlive their retirement savings."

options; we think about investing; we research investment options, meet with professionals, sacrifice certain creature comforts, and basically spend decades planning for this one specific event.

There's a reason for this focus and immense sacrifice of time and money; retirement planning is an intricate process. It involves saving to provide an income for an undetermined number of years after you stop working. That could mean five years, 10 years, 20 years—decades—depending on when you decide to retire and how long you live after that.

For most savers, the process of saving for retirement is ridiculously complex. Not only is it a sophisticated, complicated task with many different levels of consideration, it's also a minefield rife with the potential for errors that can bring devastating hardships to you and your spouse during your most financially exposed time ever: your retirement years.

In the process of saving, an investor must consider the different types of retirement savings accounts they can choose from. Their options include 401(k), Roth and Traditional IRAs, 403(b)s and annuities (which can also be within an IRA). Investors must also measure the various benefits of each, such as tax-deductible contributions, contribution limits, vesting requirements, employer matches and so on. With all the outside financial uncertainty facing retirees, most recently illustrated with talk of the fiscal cliff and the national debt hitting its cap, it's no wonder that their number-one fear is that they will outlive their retirement savings.

But physicians aren't like regular individuals. Their well-earned, high-income status has turned into a double-edged sword. Not only will it increase their tax rate both before retirement (thus giving them less income to save) and after retirement (thus reducing the effectiveness of what they do save), but it will also affect what they can and can't invest in a retirement account.

For example, a Roth IRA, which offers tax-free gains and income after retirement, is generally off limits to those who earn more than $127,000 as singles and $188,000 for married couples filing jointly (as of 2013), unless they jump through certain hoops.

These individuals can take a Traditional IRA, but between the forced distributions at age 70.5 and the $5,500 annual contribution limit (as of 2013) with a $1,000 allowable catch-up contribution for those over age 50, this will barely make a dent in your need for accumulation.

One better solution for physicians is the SEP IRA for self-employed physicians. This allows for up to $51,000 in contributions per year and another $1,000 for those over age 50. However, this still begs the question of where to invest that annual contribution. You have to invest aggressively enough that its growth can at least keep up with inflation, but not so risky that you could lose it all. Also, the SEP IRA requires a distribution at age 70.5, which is sure to bump up your income and taxes, whether you need it or not.

In the past, many physicians were unable to participate in Roth IRAs, which allow for tax-free growth and tax-free post-retirement income, because of the income restrictions placed on these accounts. While this is still technically true, there is a backdoor solution. The income restrictions formerly placed on Traditional IRA to Roth conversions were recently lifted, meaning that you can open a

Traditional IRA, fund it up to the annual maximum, then immediately convert it into a Roth IRA regardless of your income. Then, every year, you can continue to fund that Roth with after-tax dollars and secure your tax-free growth and postretirement income.

Now, if you're already feeling anxious or if you're in over your head, consider this—all we've done is discuss what you need to think about to select an account in which your retirement savings should grow. That's it—just choosing an account.

Once a saver has chosen an account, the process isn't done yet. No matter what kind of retirement account you as an investor select, you must next choose underlying investments within the account. These are the stocks, bonds, CDs, mutual funds, annuities and other investments that will sink or swim your retirement plans. Sadly, as we discussed in Chapter 3, most often these investment options sink the plans—an unwelcome reality that you can't ignore.

Truly, the decision about what to invest in, and what *not* to invest in, is one that can help or hurt your ability to retire more than any other, which is why you must make sure to take your goals for retirement into consideration before deciding.

Investment Risks

Investment risks aren't just limited to risks of loss from uncertain, high-risk investments. Retirement savers can face risks from fixed products too—such as:

- **Interest rate risk:** The risk that an investor will get locked into a noncompetitive interest rate.

- **Inflation risk:** The risk that the fixed interest rate won't keep pace with inflation.

- **Reinvestment risk:** The chance that earnings and principal won't be able to be reinvested at a competitive or comparable rate upon a fixed investment's maturity.

Risk versus Return

Risk and return. They sound good together, don't they? Almost as if they go together? That's because they *do*. Every investment option—from fixed products, such as certificates of deposit (CDs) and variable products, such as mutual funds, to sophisticated products like forward contracts or call-and-put options—

carries some level of risk. Unfortunately, the amount of risk each investment choice carries is almost always directly proportionate to the amount of return an investor can possibly earn from it.

But let's not forget that the word *risk* has a negative connotation; as you can see from the chart below, while high-risk investments offer the greatest possibility for gains, they also have the highest likelihood of loss.

How Risky is Your Portfolio?

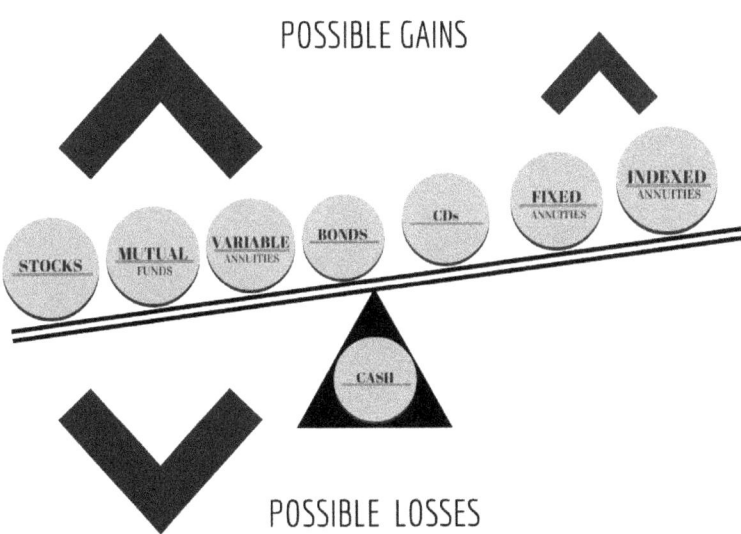

Chart courtesy of Postema Insurance & Investments, LLC. Chart reflects potential gains and potential losses of various investments and is not meant to be a guarantee or promise of performance.

When saving for retirement, an investor must be able to marry risk and return with some level of principal protection and retention. Without growth, an investor can generally not expect to accumulate enough funds to actually retire with. Without principal protection, that investor will be in an even worse position because they will lose the very financial foundation created by their savings. Without that, there is nothing left to grow returns on and nothing to draw an income from after retirement. When you're young and still climbing the career ladder, you may be able to afford to take the kind of risk that could decimate your savings principal—but the closer you get to retirement, the fewer working years you have and the less time you have to re-accumulate lost savings.

It sounds complex and dangerous—like skating over not-quite-frozen water—but it doesn't have to be. If you want it to be simple and secure, you can just use the portfolio risk illustration on the previous page to help you weigh the potential risks and returns each investment option gives you. Not only does it simplify things, but it can also save so much heartache.

The key, as this picture illustrates and you will learn more about a little later in this presentation, is to find a product that combines a suitable amount of risk with some guaranteed return and principal protection, as well as the opportunity for impressive gains—one that allows you exposure to the upside potential investors in the past few decades have enjoyed, but that also insulates you from market risk completely.

Unanticipated Expenses

If you could anticipate every expense you'll face after retirement, you'd probably also have the power to run out and get a winning lottery ticket that ensured you never needed to anticipate those expenses. If you can do that, please put this book down and do so—when you get back, I'll help you figure out how to hold onto those lottery winnings. Still here? I thought so. The sad fact is that no one knows exactly what expenses he or she might face after settling into the nonworking part of life.

There are some expenses you can reasonably expect, such as utilities and groceries. Two expenses that you can't exactly anticipate and thus accurately budget for, but you know will affect your retirement income, are inflation and taxes.

INFLATION

There has probably been at least one relative in your life who was fond of saying, "Why, when I was your age, a loaf of bread cost half of what it does now!" Heck, you might have even caught yourself saying that very thing, accompanied by an indignant shake of your head at the price surges on so many basic necessities.

Inflation is a nasty combination of an increase in prices and a decrease in the purchasing power of money. When you are working during a period of inflation, you might receive a cost-of-living increase in your salary, or you may take on a second job or work overtime at your main place of employment.

But when you retire, there are few options for dealing with inflation on your fixed savings—unless you have an annuity with certain built-in protections.

TAXES

It stings when you learn that the government is standing by, ready to take a bite out of your postretirement income. But sting or not, they are there, with a tax bill in hand. When you're just a few years out from retirement, you can work with a planner to estimate what your tax liability might be, based on current tax rates and your anticipated income from your retirement savings, pension and Social Security.

But you don't know how much that liability will grow over the next 10 or 20 years. You can, however, plan ahead with certain protections built into annuity products that can at least defer your tax penalty.

Medical Care

The presence of Medicare as a means to help retirees with their postretirement medical expenses doesn't absolve them from having any out-of-pocket medical expenses. In fact, as I mentioned in Chapter 2, couples age 65 retiring in 2012 can expect to spend as much as $240,000 out of their own pocket for their medical expenses after retirement.

To put that into perspective, the $240,000 is a 4 percent increase from the 2011 estimate, and represents a 6 percent average annual increase from 2002 estimates.[5]

If you've got years—or decades—stretching our before you retire, you could be facing an extreme increase in the amount you should expect to pay for medical care during retirement. At an average of 6 percent per year—or even a generous estimate of 4 percent per year—you could anticipate spending $300,000 or more, even with the help of Medicare. And, as most physicians know, some talented practitioners are opting out of the Medicare system, forcing seniors to pay higher rates in order to visit the doctors they want to see.

If that weren't scary enough, consider the fact that these numbers don't include nursing home care. If Social Security only increases annually by about 2 percent for cost of living adjustments, it will be no help against the rampant increase in health expenses and nursing home expenses that the average retiree faces, which is why they must look for another product to help protect their savings and their income throughout retirement.

Long-Term Care

Long-term care is one of those heavily misunderstood topics that can spell real tragedy for a retiree. Often, when planning for retirement, people neglect to consider the cost for assistance with a very specific set of needs, called activities of daily living. These activities can include dressing, showering, eating and other nonmedical actions that help foster a healthy, comfortable life. In 2012 a *Wall Street Journal* article mentioned that about 70 percent of individuals who reach 65 will need some help with these activities on a long-term basis.

This is where the confusion comes in. It's not hard to understand that you may need help with some activities, like cleaning, when you get older—but did you know that Medicare doesn't provide any kind of coverage for these expenses? That's right—if you need nonmedical assistance to keep up with the very basic activities necessary for a happy, healthy, comfortable life—then you are going to have to pay out of pocket for them after retirement.

So how much can this kind of care and assistance eat into your retirement savings? Long-term care in-home and at a facility can cost as much as $250 per day and often, once it's needed, it's needed for life.

Long-term care insurance policies allow pre- and postretirees to keep their retirement savings sheltered from the costs of long-term care needs. These policies allow the policyholder to select a waiting period between the time their need for care sets in and their policy begins paying for it, and to select the type of care they want (in-home or nursing facility). Policies of this variety can also provide further protection for inflation.

Without long-term care insurance, some low-income retirees may qualify for Medicaid, but those who've worked hard to accumulate the proper funds to support themselves through retirement will find that their savings are quickly bled away paying for care costs as their options for future living situations become more and more limited. Further, any chance of leaving a legacy for their heirs is completely obliterated.

Outliving Retirement Savings

Whether through saving too little, investing too conservatively or incorrectly assessing postretirement expenses, the bottom-line fear of every retiree is that they will outlive their retirement.

In the next section, we're going to talk about the one way that you, as a pre- or postretiree, can actually insure yourself against outliving a retirement savings through investment in annuities. Right now, let's see what James and Sharon were most concerned about when designing their retirement plan.

The Story of James and Sharon

When James was just a few months away from retirement, he checked his 401(k) account balance and then frowned in frustration. This account was supposed to comfortably support him and Sharon for decades, yet in the past three months it had fallen from $1,800,000 to $1,215,000.

James and Sharon needed to pull at least $80,000 from their savings each year, and with a rapidly falling balance, there was no way they could expect to do that for decades.

James was beginning to wonder if he would even be able to retire. And changes in the tax rates weren't doing him any favors. Add to this the pressures of creating a legacy, and James suddenly felt that retirement was the most irresponsible move he could possibly make right now.

- How do James and Sharon's experience in losing money mirror your own?

- Do you share some of the same concerns as James and Sharon?

In the next chapter, we'll start seeing how James and Sharon were able to utilize an indexed annuity with a guaranteed minimum income rider to turn this troubling situation around.

Chapter 5

Better Retirement Planning with Annuities

I know that it's frustrating to realize what little control we have over all of the challenges, pitfalls and real-life concerns of pre- and postretirees. But if you've gotten this far—if you've stuck with it even though it made you concerned or uncomfortable—then you're already ahead of the game. You've already gone farther than so many will, and that gives you a much better chance at retirement planning success than many of your peers. As unfortunate as that is for them, it means that you should move forward with your head high and hope swelling in your chest because right here—in this chapter—I'm going to introduce you to a potential solution for all the dangers we discussed in previous chapters. I'm going to introduce you to the power and flexibility of annuities.

Most of the problems and planning pitfalls we've been discussing, including the very restrictive income limitations and contribution limits for funding retirement plans and the tax-increasing forced distributions, can be resolved by using annuities in your retirement plan.

What Are Annuities?

At the most basic level,

Annuity Funding Options

There are a couple of different ways to fund the principal annuity payment.

- **Single premium:** Should a saver want to fund an annuity with one lump sum, they would have a single premium annuity. They can then choose deferred or immediate payouts.

- **Flexible premium:** Savers can make multiple payments over the course of many years in order to fund their annuity.

think of annuities as longevity insurance. They are contractual accounts issued by life insurance companies that protect against the risk of outliving your retirement savings.

You can think of annuities as a savings vehicle with an edge; while they hold your principal investment and pay interest or allow it to grow through investment in subaccounts, annuities also offer many ways in which the annuitant (one who owns the annuity and is entitled to payouts) can be paid an annual income from the principal and growth for a certain number of years or for life.

But the benefits of annuities don't stop there. Annuities may also have death benefits, guarantees and minimums built into them. They are also tax deferred, which means that the money inside an annuity grows without being taxable until the annuitant begins receiving an income.

Types of Annuities

Just as with life insurance, annuities come in many different shapes and sizes.

Fixed: A fixed annuity is one that offers a predetermined, guaranteed interest rate for the principal funds. This rate can reset from year to year.

Multi-Year Guaranteed: The MYGA is also referred to as a CD annuity. It guarantees an interest rate for an entire term, just as a CD might. However, with this annuity, one can transfer assets through a 1035 exchange and take advantage of a new annuity contract without paying taxes on the gains—something a CD can't offer.

Variable: Instead of guaranteeing a certain interest rate on the annuity principal, variable annuities have subaccounts that allow for investments in things such as stocks with a varying degree of risk based on the subaccount's underlying investments. When subaccounts underperform, an annuitant can end up with no growth on their investment.

Indexed: The indexed annuity is a sign that the insurance industry finally understood what pre- and postretirees were concerned about—finding the fragile balance between protecting their principal and exposing their savings to all the upside potential in the market. Indexed annuities have subaccounts, sometimes called buckets, with underlying investments grouped in order to model various indices. That means that they are structured to replicate the performance of a particular index, such as the S&P 500, Dow Jones

Industrial Average or the NASDAQ. A conservative choice with plenty of upside potential, an indexed annuity will also have a protection in place, called a "floor" that guarantees an investor a certain return, even if the index in their subaccount is underperforming. Likewise, they have a "ceiling" that maximizes the return an investor will receive. This mixes the best part of a variable annuity with the best part of a fixed annuity to create a savings vehicle perfect for both risk-taking and risk-averse savers.

Immediate: One of the powerful things about annuities for retirement savers is that they aren't just for the long-term planners. An immediate annuity is one that begins making payouts right after being funded.

Deferred: A deferred annuity is one that is funded, and then goes through an accumulation period, during which the premiums grow in value. Eventually, it can annuitize (although that isn't always necessary) and begin making payments. Deferred annuities may be funded in many flexible payments or one single payment and the payouts can be influenced heavily by the presence of an income rider, which is discussed in more detail in the next section.

Split-Funded Annuity: Retirement savers who want the growth power of a deferred annuity but who also need an immediate source of income can consider a split-funded annuity. With this contract, the saver determines what portion of his principal is applied to the immediate annuity and which portion goes untouched in the deferred annuity. The amount chosen for each plan will determine just how much the immediate annuity pays out and how high the accumulation and future payouts can be for the deferred. Often, the deferred annuity can grow enough to replace the amount of the original principal that was paid to the immediate annuity. Another benefit of this strategy is that, because the immediate annuity is not allowed time to grow significantly, much of it isn't taxable when paid out since it's simply a return of principal (assuming the annuity is not purchased inside a Traditional IRA).

MIXING ANNUITY FEATURES

When designing your annuity, you can take many of the options discussed in this section and the next to build your own individual savings and retirement funding vehicle.

For example, you can buy an immediate annuity, fund it with a single premium, and end up with a SPIA (single premium immediate annuity).

Annuity Riders

Annuities themselves are simple products without a lot of moving parts, but many insurers provide special additional benefits that can be added to an annuity in the form of a rider. When added to the annuity, a rider becomes a contractual obligation and will create an added cost to the annuity, which puts a little less of your principal to work— but as you can see from some of the rider benefits outlined below, the cost is far outweighed by the many important living and death benefits they provide. Some of the rider options you can select are listed on the next page.

Please note that only general information can be given for each rider. Your insurance company will have its own terminology and stipulations for rider benefits. It's important that you read your individual contract to understand how the benefits provided in your rider work. The riders mentioned here might not be a perfect fit for every individual, so make sure your advisor explains each of these additional options in depth, as well as how each may help your situation.

Cost-of-living adjustment (COLA) rider: Annuities have a certain payout amount that an annuitant can rely on. But over time, as inflation increases the price of everything a retiree needs in order to live, that payout seems less and less powerful. A cost-of-living adjustment rider, depending on the issuing insurance company, can provide a regular increase in payouts that is meant to keep up with inflation.

Guaranteed minimum accumulation benefit (GMAB) rider: This rider ensures that your variable annuity principal will be at least a certain amount at the end of the accumulation period of the annuity. So even if your subaccounts lose money, you have a guaranteed minimum to look forward to. **It's important to note that an indexed annuity does not require a GMAB, along with the**

additional cost it brings, because a minimum guarantee is already built into the policy.

Guaranteed minimum income benefit (GMIB) rider: One of the most important riders for preretirees, the GMIB rider ensures that a certain amount of income will be paid, regardless of how the subaccounts perform.

Terminal illness rider: Allows for penalty-free withdrawals (up to limits) should the annuitant be diagnosed with a terminal illness. This will allow the annuitant to use his or her withdrawal for medical expenses and an income supplement when it is most needed.

Long-term care/nursing home rider: Like the terminal illness rider, this rider allows the annuitant penalty-free access to some of the annuity's value if he or she is confined to a nursing home or, in some cases, receiving home health care secondary to an inability to care for him- or herself.

Death benefit rider: A death benefit rider (which is now available on some fixed-index annuities) guarantees that when the annuitant of a *variable annuity* passes away, his or her heirs will receive a benefit—in many cases, at least the principal contributed to the annuity, even if the account is worth less due to the underperformance of the subaccounts—although, if the subaccounts have lost 25 to 50 percent of the original investment amount, the death benefit may also reduce that amount too. However, in an indexed annuity, you cannot lose principal in the subaccounts, so this particular benefit would be unnecessary—but not the rider itself. Some death benefit riders even provide what's called a "step-up." This term comes from the benefit being a step above cost basis or principal. With it, the annuitant's heirs receive the highest value of the annuity recorded during the last month or year.

Annuity Payout Options

Annuities provide a slew of different payout options to help you plan your postretirement income allocation perfectly. Here are four of the most commonly used:

Period certain: This option ensures that monthly benefits are paid out for a predetermined period of time, such as 20 years. The benefits will continue to be paid to heirs after the annuitant passes away. Because the period of time that benefits will be paid is certain, there is less risk.

Joint & last survivor: Joint & last survivor guarantees payouts during the life of two people. So if one spouse should pass away, the other spouse will continue to receive payments until his or her death. Joint annuities are not restricted to spouses, however, so an annuitant could name one of their heirs or a significant other as the joint annuitant.

Straight life: This option affords the highest amount of monthly income, but does have some risk. In a straight life payout, the annuity will pay you an income for life—even if you outlive the principal and earnings.

Life income with period certain: Less risky than straight life annuity payouts, this option allows for a guaranteed life income but also provides a set period of time for payouts to last after the annuitant dies, assuming the annuitant passes away before the end of the period certain term.

Guaranteed minimum income rider: When designing your annuity and your payout, you can also select a guaranteed minimum income benefit (GMIB) rider. As I mentioned in the last section, this benefit ensures that a certain amount of income will be paid out, regardless of how the subaccounts performed. This is the only option that allows you to completely avoid annuitization.

Combining this rider with a joint life annuity allows the full accumulation value to go to the beneficiary at the time of death of the first annuitant, or the joint annuitant may choose to continue taking payments.

As you can see, annuities offer a secure and flexible means of not only funding your retirement but also of creating payouts and planning around future retirement pitfalls.

They are also one of the safest investments for retirees which make them even more attractive to the average retirement saver. Finally, annuities offer savers an opportunity to

"Never invest in a business you cannot understand."
—Warren Buffett

invest in a product that they can understand—one of Warren Buffett's top tenets for investing.

But retirement planning isn't as simple as all that, and insurance companies understand the various challenges that retirees face, so they've developed products and riders that complement the basic structure of an annuity and enhance the benefits that it offers you.

Annuity Payout Options

It's one thing to read the description of annuity payout options, and another to actually look at some numbers and see how the different payout options affect payments, especially since the wrong annuity can do a retiree more harm than good as it ties up principal savings in exchange for a very low annual payment.

Let's consider a $1,000,000 single premium immediate annuity (SPIA) purchased by a 65-year-old and his wife. It is a joint life annuity with a 10-year period certain, which means payments continue for whichever is longer—the 10-year period or the death of the final living spouse. Payments are set to begin one month after the annuity is purchased.

Okay, let's queue the drum roll to see what kind of annual payment we're looking at. Ready?

It's:

$56,999.51 per year

Preretirees must be extremely careful in selecting the right annuity to supplement their income in their retirement years. The joint life with period certain annuity above doesn't necessarily offer the most effective, flexible plan for retirement savings and the most potential for return on invested principal. There is one product with an intrinsic means of creating great returns, protecting against losses through market exposure, and making annual payments that can actually change how a retiree affords to live, without eradicating the legacy the retiree may want to leave. That is an *indexed annuity with guaranteed income benefit and death benefit riders*.

In the next section, we're going to examine the actual mechanics of designing your annuity for retirement. In doing so, we're going to focus on the important annuity structures and benefits that can really give your retirement planning an edge by providing guarantees, impressive growth potential with minimal risk, and protections to help you merge retirement planning with capital retention and legacy protection. With the indexed annuity, death benefit rider and guaranteed minimum income rider, I am going to show you how to easily create a retirement portfolio that is unrivaled in other planning products for both safety and upside potential. Not only that, but you can also adjust when you decide to take payments through an income rider and have even more control over your money and your income, which is one of the reasons income riders are gaining in popularity over single premium immediate annuities.

For a preview of how the indexed annuity with riders can work for your retirement, let's check back in with James and Sharon and see how this annuity is working for them.

The Story of James and Sharon

Sharon was unhappy when James finally decided to delay his retirement. She demanded they consult a professional first, and that's when they came in to see me.

Based on their savings and postretirement income needs, we agreed they would be the perfect fit for a 10-year indexed annuity with a 5 percent bonus up front. Because the bonus was paid up front, it was able to start earning along with their principal deposit of $1,215,000.

The minimum guaranteed income their annuity paid them was $75,794 per year, which meant, with Social Security, they had more than they needed each year. And like Social Security, this annuity payment was for life—guaranteed.

Because they didn't annuitize, they simply activated their guaranteed income rider; when both James and Sharon pass away, their children will receive 100 percent of the accumulation value at death.

Chapter 6

Indexed Annuities

Every investor has a secret dream. He or she may not share it with others, but it likely plays on the edges of their mind at some point throughout the day, week or month when they look at their investment account balances. That dream is of enjoying all the upside potential that the stock market has to offer without any—or much—of the risks: to have the principal earning money when the market is in an upswing but to also enjoy total protection from the worst of any downswings that follow. Not every saver can boast such an innovative retirement plan design, but those with indexed annuities can.

What Is an Indexed Annuity?

An indexed annuity is a savings contract that allows your invested principal to grow based on the performance of a chosen subaccount, which is modeled to perform like a stock index, such as NASDAQ, S&P 500, the Dow Jones Industrial Average, or the Russell 2000. The subaccounts are designed to mimic the movement of the market over time; if the market rises, so does the value of the annuity.

This growth pattern makes the interest rate and potential gains of an indexed annuity variable, but these contracts have protections built into them that guarantee a minimum return on the principal, so savers never need to feel as though they are going to lose money from market exposure. By the same token, they never feel as though they are giving up healthy gains by limiting market exposure.

Indexed annuities have the same payout and funding options as other annuities and can have many of the same riders. When a saver combines the indexed annuity with the guaranteed minimum income rider (discussed in the next chapter), they can create a trifecta of retirement benefits:

- Access to competitive gains
- Complete protection from market risks
- Guaranteed income

The Value of Accumulation

When you think about retirement savings as an abstract concept, and not one you are emotionally and financially dependent upon, it's pretty absurd:

1. During your working life, you make a certain income every year.

2. You are supposed to set a portion of that income aside to use later on when you are no longer working.

3. When you retire, you should have saved enough money out of your annual income to have built up a new, postretirement income for all the years that you live.

> *"Rule No. 1: Never lose money. Rule No. 2: Never forget rule No. 1."*
> *—Warren Buffett*

When you look at it like that, it's easy to see that it's impossible to simply set your money under the mattress and expect to have set enough aside by age 65 to retire and support yourself for the rest of your life.

The key to a successful retirement plan is mixing savings with healthy accumulation and then adding in certain income guarantees—all of which are accomplished by the indexed annuity with the guaranteed minimum income rider.

The income rider is especially helpful to physicians who often see their work as a calling, not a job, and therefore wish to remain working far into what are traditionally considered retirement years. The GMIB rider allows the physician to choose when to activate the income stream so that he or she is not forced to take it while still working.

THE POWER AND DRAWBACKS OF ACCUMULATION

Accumulation—the growth of your principal—is a vital component of a successful retirement plan. But you've got to pay in order to play, and that payment often comes in the form of the risk of a complete and utter loss of your principal investment.

Think about the many investors who bet on supposedly solid companies in the past 20 years. Those who invested their 401(k)s in the stock of the company they worked for that eventually went bankrupt, or who lost everything during the '90s tech bubble or the 2008 recession.

And yet, even with all of this risk, savers absolutely must find a way to help their savings grow and accumulate in order to accommodate increasing retirement expenses and life spans. Then, eventually, they must switch their mindsets to preservation and distribution mode—but they must have assets in order to do that.

Continued …

Let's look at some simple numbers that illustrate just how important accumulation is. The following charts compare a $1,200 per year savings over 21 years with and without interest:

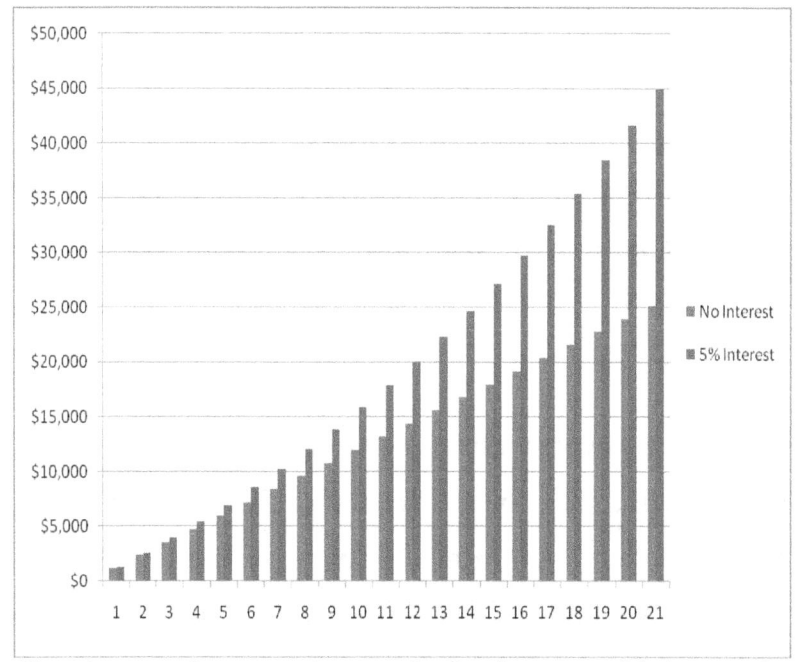

Chart shows an ultraconservative example of performance and is for example purposes only. It is not meant to guarantee a payout or return.

Indexed Annuities: Accumulation, Guarantees and Upside Potential

We know that accumulation is vital to a retirement plan, and we understand that being cautious and conservative is important, but let's talk about how being overly cautious can hurt and how indexed annuities offer the perfect marriage among accumulation, protection and guarantees.

When dealing with a fixed product, investors have a pretty clear picture of what their growth will be. They know that if their fixed investment grows at 2 percent per year for five years, they will gain a certain amount of money. But what investors don't know is how much they will *lose* by investing in fixed products, locking in a low rate and missing out on what the growth in the market can offer—which is exactly why an indexed annuity may have an advantage over a traditional, fixed annuity.

To illustrate the difference, let's look at two annuity illustrations. First, we have a fixed annuity with an initial deposit of $500,000 growing at a rate of 3 percent for five years and thereafter:

2014

Attained Age	Principal	Interest Rate	Total Value
55	$500,000	3.00%	$515,000
56	$500,000	3.00%	$530,450
57	$500,000	3.00%	$546,365
58	$500,000	3.00%	$562,755
59	$500,000	3.00%	$579,635
60	$500,000	3.00%	$597,025
61	$500,000	3.00%	$614,935
62	$500,000	3.00%	$633,385
63	$500,000	3.00%	$652,385
64	$500,000	3.00%	$671,960
65	$500,000	3.00%	$692,115
66	$500,000	3.00%	$712,880
67	$500,000	3.00%	$734,265
68	$500,000	3.00%	$756,295

Illustration is for sample purposes only. It is not meant to represent a guarantee of your individual performance.

Now, let's look at that same $500,000 if it had been invested in an indexed annuity with a 5 percent cap and subaccounts that mimicked the performance of the Dow Jones Industrial Average:

2014

Year	Attained Age	Principal	Earned Interest	Total Value
1997	55	$500,000	27.23%	$636,168
1998	56	$500,000	8.86%	$692,531
1999	57	$500,000	16.06%	$803,768
2000	58	$500,000	0.00%	$803,768
2001	59	$500,000	0.00%	$803,768
2002	60	$500,000	0.00%	$803,768
2003	61	$500,000	0.00%	$803,768
2004	62	$500,000	12.23%	$902,068
2005	63	$500,000	1.87%	$918,896
2006	64	$500,000	3.09%	$947,275
2007	65	$500,000	22.34%	$1,158,885
2008	66	$500,000	0.00%	$1,158,885
2009	67	$500,000	0.00%	$1,158,885
2010	68	$500,000	19.08%	$1,379,986

Illustration is for sample purposes only. It is not meant to represent a guarantee of your individual performance.

As you can see, even in years during which the DJIA fell (including in 2009 when it fell over 30 percent), our example annuitant lost nothing and gained significantly more than the annuitant in the fixed annuity. In this particular example, the index was averaged monthly point-to-point, which results in a high return for the annuity owner, showing that even with a mindset of erring on the side of investment safety, you can enjoy some really nice years of growth while others are dealing with losses.

Let's look at another indexed annuity example with monthly point-to-point averaging, this one with a subaccount that mimics the S&P 500:

Year	Attained Age	Principal	Earned Interest	Total Value
1997	55	$500,000	25.28%	$626,386
1998	56	$500,000	17.96%	$738,884
1999	57	$500,000	14.86%	$848,681
2000	58	$500,000	0.08%	$849,350
2001	59	$500,000	0.00%	$849,350
2002	60	$500,000	0.00%	$849,350
2003	61	$500,000	0.00%	$849,350
2004	62	$500,000	13.72%	$965,883
2005	63	$500,000	6.36%	$1,027,344
2006	64	$500,000	2.15%	$1,049,412
2007	65	$500,000	21.70%	$1,277,140
2008	66	$500,000	0.00%	$1,277,140
2009	67	$500,000	0.00%	$1,277,140
2010	68	$500,000	17.18%	$1,496,566

Illustration is for sample purposes only. It is not meant to represent a guarantee of your individual performance.

While the actual performance of your indexed annuity may not deliver a return that is high year after year, you can at least see the difference between your accumulation potential with the indexed annuity and the limitations of the fixed annuity.

Of course, the other benefit of an indexed annuity is that while you have all that upside potential and market exposure, you also have the benefit of a guaranteed return when your subaccounts don't do as well as you'd like. The same cannot be said for a variable annuity, which can create substantial losses that can ruin your chances for retirement. It just goes to show that you don't have to bet the farm to reap rewards like you used to.

That's right—a variable annuity can create substantial losses. That means you could put your savings in a variable annuity and, if the investments within your subaccounts or the market as a whole takes a downturn, you could be looking not only at a lack of savings accumulation but an actual reduction in the value of your annuity and the savings you put toward it.

In 2011 Morningstar released a report that showed 99 percent of the conservative variable annuity subaccounts—money fund subaccounts—had negative returns in the preceding 12 months.[10] So if one of the most conservative subaccount options in a variable annuity can perform that badly, how much could be lost when investing in the mid- to high-risk subaccounts?

In a worst-case scenario, a variable annuity doesn't just "not grow"—it can lose some of the precious assets you deposit into it. Can you afford to risk your retirement so completely?

There is no question that the combination of downside protection and upside potential in an indexed annuity makes it the go-to product for retirement savers. Where else can you ensure that you benefit from positive market activity while completely avoiding the potential for losses and securing a minimum, guaranteed return?

With a variable annuity, you don't just risk underperformance—you could face a loss in your invested capital.

In the next chapter, we're going to show you how you can give your indexed annuity an even more compelling edge through the use of a guaranteed minimum income benefit (GMIB) rider.

Taxes and Indexed Annuities

While securing your principal at the same time you guarantee a minimum return and retain the benefit of exposure to market upturns are the main features of an indexed annuity, let's not forget about the potential tax benefits of an annuity.

Purchased straight from the insurance company and outside of any restrictive retirement account with annual

"Gains made inside an annuity are not taxable as long as they remain in the annuity."

contribution limits, gains made inside an annuity are not taxable as long as they remain in the annuity. You can even modify the subaccounts that you invest in to better suit your risk tolerance. You can also move the funds to a different annuity through a 1035 exchange without prompting a tax bill.*

*A 1035 exchange can result in surrender charges or create a new surrender period for your funds.

When purchased in an IRA, annuity premiums can be tax-deductible (provided you meet the phase out limits); however, savers must be careful to consider all the ramifications of an IRA before they decide to purchase their annuity inside of one. There could be additional penalties for early withdrawal, stiff contribution limits and required minimum withdrawals at a certain age.

For some, a Roth IRA proves a better option. With a Roth IRA, your contributions are not tax-deductible, but the distributions you take (when qualified) are tax-free, as is the growth of the account balance, as long as it remains in the IRA. Once again, however, Roth IRAs have contribution limits, additional penalties for nonqualified withdrawals and income limits that can mean that most physicians won't qualify.

Roth IRA Conversion

It's not uncommon to start out with your annuity in a Traditional IRA and then realize at some point in the future that a Roth IRA would be more desirable. Often, this occurs because savers realize that the tax break given for

Traditional IRA contributions (which may only be partially deductible) is not as powerful as the ability to take a tax-free income at retirement. Remember, your tax bracket may be significantly less at retirement than it is while you're working, but you'll be taking years and years of tax-deferred growth out of the Traditional IRA, which can add up to a significant amount to pay taxes on. Additionally, even if you don't need to withdraw from your IRA because you have other sources of postretirement income, a Traditional IRA forces distributions after you reach age 70.5, which also triggers an increase in your tax liability.

Luckily, you aren't necessarily locked in to your Traditional IRA if you decide that a Roth is a better fit. In 2010 the $100,000 income limit for Roth IRA conversions was lifted, allowing more pre- and postretirees to make a change in account type, which can have a drastic effect on the longevity of their retirement savings.

When converting a Traditional IRA to a Roth IRA, some tax correction must occur. The IRS will expect you to pay taxes on the current value of deductible IRA funds that you convert. It's important that you have the available funds to pay these taxes; if you take them out of the IRA to pay, then not only will you reduce the amount of your investment you have earning for you but there will also be additional penalties incurred if you are under the age of 59.5.

Another consideration to make before converting from a Traditional to a Roth is that you must allow the Roth to be untouched for five years before you can take qualified distributions—even if you are over the age of 59.5. So if you want to convert, but also need to take distributions now, you may need an alternative solution.

If either the tax liability or the waiting period is a problem, you can always consider a partial conversion—or several of them—so that you can gradually move your money over without having to incur the taxes all in one fell swoop. This also allows you the opportunity to continue distributions from the Traditional IRA during the five-year waiting period for the Roth.

The Stretch IRA

Whenever an investor opens an IRA, he or she must choose a beneficiary to pass the account onto in the event of death.

The beneficiary, in turn, must take a Required Minimum Distribution (assuming the IRA is Traditional) based on their age—which means the older the beneficiary is, the more they will be forced to take from the IRA every year. For some, such as a spouse who is the same age as the deceased IRA holder, that could mean they are forced to take more income than they need, and therefore forced to pay more in taxes than they want or can afford. In addition, this can drastically, and quickly, reduce the balance in the IRA, leaving less money growing and increasing the size of the beneficiary's taxable estate.

In order to stretch out the number of generations the IRA balance can touch and the amount of time the principal can grow, some IRA accountholders choose to name a child or grandchild as the beneficiary instead of a spouse. This is considered a stretch and is a valid option for legacy planning.

Diversification and Indexed Annuities

If there is one thing that financial gurus the world over agree on, it's that diversification is a vital component to any saver's plan. Diversification is the process of investing in many different

"Diversification is the process of investing in many different types of savings vehicles, risk classes and industries in order to reduce risk."

types of savings vehicles, risk classes and industries in order to reduce risk of loss in your portfolio.

Diversification acts as a buffer against loss by ensuring that you don't have all your eggs in a single basket. That way, if one of your investments begins to go south, your other investments may still be growing, thereby stemming the damage of the failing investment.

But diversification doesn't just hedge against risk; it can also increase exposure to gains. If you invest all your money into one vehicle or industry, you are limited to the gains that particular investment brings. When you stretch your savings across multiple buckets, you create all kinds of new opportunities for savings growth.

Indexed annuities are the definitive tool for easy diversification because they offer you many different options for your underlying investments. Some even have up to 13 different subaccounts to choose from—and you can change your selections every year at the contract anniversary so that as your risk tolerance changes or you identify underperforming subaccounts, you can make the appropriate adjustments with no fees.

"Indexed annuities are the definitive tool for easy diversification because they offer you many different options for your underlying investments."

An indexed annuity makes diversification simple and effective and gives it an additional benefit that no other investment can offer—even while an annuitant is diversifying and looking at varying levels of risk in their subaccounts, they still benefit from the guarantees within the annuity itself, as well as those in the income rider.

Death Benefits and Indexed Annuities

Annuities may be there to provide an income after you've retired and guard you against outliving your retirement savings, but for many with children and grandchildren, the thought of also providing a legacy is vitally important. Luckily, annuities have you covered there as well—but you must add a death benefit rider* for them to be truly covered the way you want them to be.

*For individuals in good health, a life insurance policy may be a better option, so be sure to discuss that possibility with your advisor.

The type of death benefit your heirs receive can also depend on the type of annuity you purchase. For example, a variable annuity may have an account value well below the initial principal, which means that the annuitant's heirs—if they receive anything—will suffer from market exposure and losses. But that is not so with an indexed annuity.

In the following example, you can see what the death benefit on an indexed annuity with a guaranteed minimum death benefit rider looks like:

Initial Premium:	$1,000,000		
Premium Bonus:	10%		
Attained Age	End of Year	Bonus Credit	Death Benefit
66	1	5%	$1,155,000
67	2	5%	$1,212,750
68	3	5%	$1,273,390
69	4	5%	$1,337,060
70	5	5%	$1,403,910
71	6	5%	$1,474,110
72	7	5%	$1,547,810
73	8	5%	$1,625,200
74	9	5%	$1,706,460
75	10	5%	$1,791,780
76	11	6%	$1,899,290
77	12	6%	$2,013,250
78	13	6%	$2,134,040
79	14	6%	$2,200,000

The above illustration is for sample purposes only. It is not meant to be a guarantee of your individual performance.

No need to worry about losses in the market or forced annuitization taking away money from your heirs. Instead, you get a guaranteed death benefit that grows over time!

Of course, many annuities can pay full accumulation at death, which makes it important to discuss with your agent. When you do, he or she may suggest that you look at a death benefit rider.

As we discussed in Chapter 5, death benefit riders guarantee that your heirs can receive a death benefit based on the value of your annuity after you die.

Depending on the rider and the insurance company, in a variable annuity, that benefit may be equal to the principal contributed to the annuity, a reduced amount based on reduced value of underlying subaccounts, or an amount that is above the principal, based on the highest value of the annuity during the past month or year.

Legacy planning is important for many consumers but with a traditional retirement account, such as an IRA, it can be difficult to live off the saved funds while preserving some of the assets for your heirs. Indexed annuities with a guaranteed income benefit rider and/or a death benefit rider allow you to meet your postretirement needs while still providing a legacy for your children, grandchildren and other heirs.

We know how James and Sharon fixed their retirement income issues, so let's meet another couple—Chad and

Regina—who already had an annuity, but not the *right* annuity.

Chad and Regina

Chad and Regina were both still working professionals in the medical community. They were active at their local country club, took vacations away with friends, handled all their bills, invested in real estate and still put away a substantial amount into their savings accounts—or, they had been until the year they came to see me. That year, with the price of gas, food and almost everything else rising, Chad and Regina were concerned. They noticed they were actually taking money out of their savings every month in order to make ends meet, and the market wasn't picking up any of the slack for them with what remained invested.

Of course, it wasn't just their retirement savings that were dropping; the variable annuity they bought in 2005 was also losing money every year. So much so, they'd actually lost some of the principal.

Continued…

That's when they came to me for advice, completely unsure if their situation was even redeemable. We helped them roll their variable annuity's $300,000 balance into an indexed annuity, utilizing a 1035 exchange to avoid taxes. They immediately received a 5 percent bonus, helping to replenish some of their losses.

Then, we added a guaranteed minimum income rider so that they'd receive an annual income of $29,705 beginning at age 55. Even better, that payment is for life, no matter how the market performs. And that's the net amount they'll receive with taxes withheld.

Chapter 7

Guaranteed Income Benefit

Your safe money strategy employing an indexed annuity would not be complete without the guaranteed income benefit rider.

Why You Need It

Guaranteed minimum income benefit (GMIB) riders are only recently available for indexed annuities, and they're sort of like wrapping a guarantee around a guarantee. While an indexed annuity on its own may be right for you—especially if you're looking for accumulation—adding a GMIB rider can supercharge the benefit for some. The rider ensures that, once activated, you receive a certain annual payout or withdrawal based on your age at the time you want withdrawals to begin. In that respect, it is similar to Social

Security in that the later you choose to activate the payments, the larger your guaranteed payout will be.

One of the most powerful aspects of this rider is that you never have to activate the GMIB benefit—as long as you buy it outside of a Traditional IRA, an account that imposes annual minimum distribution requirements once you reach 70.5 years of age. And even if you activate the guaranteed minimum income rider, the annuity doesn't annuitize (begin to pay out in one of the ways we discussed in Chapter 5), so your money can just sit and grow, or you can pull out a lump sum. With an income rider, you can even turn the income benefit on and off as you—and your budget—sees fit. It is still important, however, to beware of advisors who explain this in a vague way or who tell you it's a guaranteed percentage for a set number of years. This implies that your return or accumulation will be that good, which is not necessarily the case since the 6 percent is only growing on your benefit base.

With a GMIB rider, you gain four points of power that very few savers, investors or retirees enjoy.

- **Absolutely NO downside risks:** Unlike a 401(k) or IRA with underlying investments, the indexed annuity ensures that you have no exposure to market risks and investment losses. The GMIB rider ensures that you have a guaranteed income of a fixed percentage. Your death benefit rider ensures that you have something to pass on to your heirs. Even without the rider, you still receive full accumulation value at death.

- **Guaranteed income FOR LIFE:** With any other type of retirement plan, you can outlive your income. And if the market tanks, it will wipe out

  "No matter how your subaccounts perform, you can rely on getting that payment for the rest of your life ..."

  your savings before you've even had a chance to outlive them.

- **Investment flexibility:** You can choose the subaccounts and risk tolerance you are most comfortable with because you retain full control over the account. This gives you the power to change your mind if life throws a curve ball.

- **Control:** It's your annuity—you decide when to activate the GMIB after waiting the required amount of time. You can also decide whether to take a lump sum, change underlying subaccounts and select your ideal beneficiary.

How It Works

This rider must be added to your annuity when you initially purchase it. There is no opportunity to change your mind later and decide it's a good idea to add it—you need to know that it's a good idea now, when you get started. With that said, you may *remove* the rider anytime.

When you add one of these riders to any kind of indexed annuity (including one that pays a bonus), you get a second set of accumulation values, which creates a base for your income benefit withdrawals. But your annuity will also show a cash value for the underlying principal growth and a surrender value, which is the amount you are entitled to if you decide not to activate the income benefit and instead withdraw a lump sum.

When you choose to activate the rider, you will begin receiving annual, monthly or quarterly payments at the percentage rate guaranteed by the rider based on the age you activate it. Then, no matter how your subaccounts perform, you can rely on getting that payment for the rest of your life—even if you live well beyond the value of your initial deposit. You can even choose a joint payout for the duration of two lives. The only factor that could negatively impact your income payments is the decision to take a withdrawal from your principal.

Some insurance companies also offer an increasing income benefit, which can raise the amount you are able to withdraw from year to year. Talk to your agent to determine if this is appropriate for your postretirement needs.

Why It Works

You might be wondering how an insurance company can guarantee that kind of payment—and guarantee it over a time period that is so uncertain. There are a few things that make this possible.

1. A premium is charged for the rider. The GMIB rider usually is not free. Your insurance company will charge you a fee, which will help offset the potential cost of the rider. (A few Index Annuity Carriers offer a free income rider.)

2. Your money has grown. Let's say that you have an income withdrawal of 4 percent. You must wait at least one year (maybe longer, depending on your insurance company—although there is at least one that provides an immediate benefit) to activate the rider. At that point, your account balance has already grown and the insurance company might have even made additional points on top of what is in your account.

3. Your money continues to grow. After you've taken the first 4 percent of your account value out in a payment, the remaining 96 percent (which may still be well above your initial principal) has another year to grow before your next withdrawal. At this rate, year after year, it would take a very, very long time to deplete your account.

In an indexed annuity with guaranteed income rider, your money grows in the background while you spend the rider withdrawal.

Fees

There is some talk about the fees associated with these riders, and as estate planners, we can appreciate that fees reduce the power of your invested dollar. But what many try to overlook when discussing these fees is that there are other products that charge fees:

o Your IRA probably has an annual fee charged by your custodian. On top of that, you pay a fee or commission for every trade you make—both buying and selling. And if you have a managed account, you are paying a management fee.

o Mutual fund fees (or the expense ratio) can be up to 2 percent each year—significantly more than your rider fee. In addition, they often have loads, which are sales fees that may be charged when you buy the mutual fund or when you sell it.

o There are often fees for the underlying investments chosen in a 401(k). Because 401(k)s fall under the Employee Retirement Income Security Act, your custodian has a lot of regulated standards to meet, which can get expensive. Those costs are passed on to you through their annual fees. You may also be charged sales fees for moving into (or out of) different investments, management fees for certain underlying investments and even fees for statements, investment advice and telephone calls to the custodian.

This is not meant to downplay the importance of maxing out your employer's 401(k) or taking advantage of the tax incentives of an IRA, but simply to illustrate that no investment is without a related expense. Your job is to make sure that you choose the investment that most effectively utilizes the fees you will be charged and offers the most value in exchange for them.

And that word—*value*—introduces the area in which indexed annuities with the guaranteed minimum income benefit (GMIB) rider have an edge over any other retirement savings vehicle out there. It's possible that you are already one step ahead of us and have been shouting out the biggest difference of all with frustration, waiting for us to mention it—so let us put you at ease and state it right now:

All retirement accounts and most investments have fees. Sometimes, you pay both an account fee AND a fee or commission for the underlying investment. But never— unless you have an indexed annuity with a GMIB—do you get any kind of *guarantees*. Even better—index annuities often have no fees unless riders are added to them, and some GMIB riders are offered for free or with a lower roll-up.

For the fees charged by the annuity—which are for the GMIB rider and may include surrender fees for early withdrawal and are often less than the fees you'd be charged for other retirement vehicles and strategies combined with transactions—you get a guaranteed income for life and a buffer against market risk that doesn't force you to give up market gains.

State Guaranty Associations, Reserves and Ratings

Here is one of the biggest hidden secrets that Wall Street and your banker hope you never find out: insurance companies issuing annuities and life insurance policies have many state-regulated requirements to maintain that help ensure that you and your investment are safe. One of these is that they must have a certain amount of money in "reserves" in order to ensure that they can meet the financial obligations associated with the policies and annuities they've issued.

Reserve requirements can be determined differently by each state. Generally, a state will determine how much is required to be set aside in reserves based on the potential claims, the number of policyholders and claims experience. Reserves are an important concept for investors and savers to grasp because they indicate that there are funds set aside in a special account just for withdrawals and claims.

A Word about Safety

Insurance companies are required to set aside a certain amount of money into *reserves* so that they can meet their financial obligations to their annuitants and policyholders.

In addition, states have set up state guaranty associations that guarantee a certain amount of cash values should an insurer become insolvent.

Another facet in consumer safety is A.M. Best ratings. A.M. Best measures the financial security of insurance companies and issues a letter rating that reflects its interpretation of the insurer's ability to make good on the promises made in its annuity and life insurance contracts. Once you have $250,000 or more to deposit into an annuity, it's a good idea to start paying attention to this letter grade. Generally, I suggest that you go with an insurer that has a B+ or higher rating.

State guaranty associations are funds made available by the states to pay those affected by an insolvent insurer. Historically, the list of failed or insolvent insurers is far less than the list of failed banks in recent years. In fact, in 2010 the National Organization of Life and Health Insurance Guaranty Associations (NOLHGA) released a list of those life and health companies that had failed between 1991 and 2010. In total, there were 70 companies listed. The Federal Deposit Insurance Corporation (FDIC), on the other hand, reports over 400 bank failures just between the years 2000 and 2012.[11, 12]

Even though insurers fail far less often than banks, state guaranty funds are there just in case, providing anywhere between $100,000 and $500,000 for annuity values held by insolvent insurers, unless that insurance was issued by a fraternal organization, since they do not have to be members of a state guaranty association. Each state has different maximums, so you should familiarize yourself with those of your state. Each of these points adds another layer of protection for your retirement and your savings.

Now, let's check in with a client of mine, Melanie, who thought she had the perfect plan for growth, safety and preservation in CDs and money market accounts—without realizing how dangerous that position was.

Melanie

When Melanie, a retired surgeon, came to me for advice five years ago, she was spending $120,000 a year just on bills and lifestyle maintenance. While some investors may be able to do this and have some of their balances bounce back with investment growth, Melanie was invested only in CDs and money market accounts at her local bank. This left her with rates so low, they couldn't even compete with inflation. Not only that, but if she needed more than she had in the money market or in recently matured CDs, she would face a penalty—a retiree's worst nightmare, and she could see it coming.

I put her in several indexed annuities with a cumulative value of $900,000. We laddered the annuities so that she could trigger the guaranteed income rider one at a time.

Now, Melanie's been taking $76,000 a year and she has more money in her annuities than she did when we first met and hasn't had to adjust her standard of living. Additionally, she has a guaranteed income for life— something that her CDs could never have given her.

Chapter 8

It's All about the Numbers

In order to show just how powerful an indexed annuity with a guaranteed minimum income benefit (GMIB) rider is, let's look at the numbers.

In this example, we have a 45-year-old who has deposited $500,000 into an indexed annuity with a bonus. He capitalized on the bonus by adding a guaranteed minimum income rider rolling up at 6.5 percent for 15 years. In this example, we're showing the amount of income he could withdraw and the way that it increases the longer he waits to take it.

2014

Years Since Annuity Purchase	Attained Age	Benefit Base	Income Withdrawal	Income Amount
6	50	$753,548	3.50%	$26,374
7	51	$802,528	3.50%	$28,088
8	52	$854,693	3.50%	$29,914
9	53	$910,248	3.50%	$31,859
10	54	$969,414	3.50%	$33,929
11	55	$1,032,426	4.00%	$41,297
12	56	$1,099,533	4.00%	$43,981
13	57	$1,171,003	4.00%	$46,840
14	58	$1,247,118	4.00%	$49,885
15	59	$1,328,181	4.00%	$53,127
16	60	$1,414,513	4.50%	$63,653
17	61	$1,414,513	4.50%	$63,653
18	62	$1,414,513	4.50%	$63,653
19	63	$1,414,513	4.50%	$63,653
20	64	$1,414,513	4.50%	$63,653
21	65	$1,414,513	5.00%	$70,726
22	66	$1,414,513	5.00%	$70,726
23	67	$1,414,513	5.00%	$70,726
24	68	$1,414,513	5.00%	$70,726

This illustration is for sample purposes only. It is not meant to be a guarantee of your individual performance. It's important to note that this illustration also assumes that no withdrawals were taken from the annuity so the principal was allowed time to grow and accumulate.

Can you imagine your retirement looking like the above example? Can you imagine knowing that, at age 65, you can begin taking over $70,000 per year—for life—and never outlive your savings? And even better, pay attention to the "benefit base" column in the middle. It shows that, should you wait to start your income, your money will *continue to grow* for up to 15 years. If the index account that the fund is using outperforms, in this case, the 6.5 percent on the benefit base, you will get the value of the index account for your new benefit base. This is called a step-up and creates almost a separate fund to access if necessary (withdrawals may reduce balances and benefits).

In the next example, we have the same 45-year-old depositing $750,000 into an indexed annuity with a bonus. Just as above, he capitalized on the bonus by adding a guaranteed minimum income rider rolling up at 6.5 percent for 15 years.

2014

Years Since Annuity Purchase	Attained Age	Benefit Base	Income Withdrawal	Income Amount
6	50	$1,130,321	3.50%	$39,561
7	51	$1,203,792	3.50%	$42,133
8	52	$1,282,039	3.50%	$44,871
9	53	$1,365,371	3.50%	$47,788
10	54	$1,454,121	3.50%	$50,894
11	55	$1,548,638	4.00%	$61,946
12	56	$1,649,300	4.00%	$65,972
13	57	$1,756,504	4.00%	$70,260
14	58	$1,870,677	4.00%	$74,827
15	59	$1,992,271	4.00%	$79,691
16	60	$2,121,769	4.50%	$95,480
17	61	$2,121,769	4.50%	$95,480
18	62	$2,121,769	4.50%	$95,480
19	63	$2,121,769	4.50%	$95,480
20	64	$2,121,769	4.50%	$95,480
21	65	$2,121,769	5.00%	$106,088
22	66	$2,121,769	5.00%	$106,088
23	67	$2,121,769	5.00%	$106,088
24	68	$2,121,769	5.00%	$106,088

This illustration is for sample purposes only. It is not meant to be a guarantee of your individual performance. It's important to note that this illustration also assumes that no withdrawals were taken from the annuity so the principal was allowed time to grow and accumulate.

Finally, let's see what happens to that withdrawal amount when the same 45-year-old deposits $1,000,000 into the same annuity with bonus.

2014

Years Since Annuity Purchase	Attained Age	Benefit Base	Income Withdrawal	Income Amount
6	50	$1,507,095	3.50%	$52,748
7	51	$1,605,057	3.50%	$56,177
8	52	$1,709,385	3.50%	$59,828
9	53	$1,820,495	3.50%	$63,717
10	54	$1,938,827	3.50%	$67,859
11	55	$2,064,851	4.00%	$82,594
12	56	$2,199,067	4.00%	$87,963
13	57	$2,342,006	4.00%	$93,680
14	58	$2,494,236	4.00%	$99,769
15	59	$2,656,362	4.00%	$106,254
16	60	$2,829,025	4.50%	$127,306
17	61	$2,829,025	4.50%	$127,306
18	62	$2,829,025	4.50%	$127,306
19	63	$2,829,025	4.50%	$127,306
20	64	$2,829,025	4.50%	$127,306
21	65	$2,829,025	5.00%	$141,451
22	66	$2,829,025	5.00%	$141,451
23	67	$2,829,025	5.00%	$141,451
24	68	$2,829,025	5.00%	$141,451

This illustration is for sample purposes only. It is not meant to be a guarantee of your individual performance. It's important to note that this illustration also assumes that no withdrawals were taken from the annuity so the principal was allowed time to grow and accumulate.

As you can see, the indexed annuity with guaranteed benefit rider offers a tremendous opportunity for securing a substantial income, for life, after retirement. The benefit becomes even more startling when you contrast it to what a

65-year-old couple depositing $1,000,000 into a single premium immediate annuity will receive—$56,999.51 for life, with a 10-year fixed period guaranteed, meaning payments continue for a total of 10 years, even if their joint deaths occur within that period. Now, would you rather receive $141,451 for life—or $56,999.51?

Many financial advisors state that in order to have a decent retirement, you must save at least 70 percent of your preretirement income for every year you live in retirement. For physicians making $200,000 or more, retiring at age 65 with a life expectancy well into their 90s, that could mean you need to have saved $4 million or more. Let's face it. The dream of saving millions of dollars while trying to support a family, build a practice or a name in your specialty, and live a life you can enjoy is just that—a dream. With the simple example above, we've shown you how you can turn just 25 percent of what the "experts" suggest into a guaranteed lifetime income that will meet that 70 percent income recommendation during your retirement years.

Now, let's take a look at a sample indexed annuity (black squares) against the growth and dips in the S&P 500 index from 1998 to 2011 (dark grey circles) and putting your money under your mattress (light grey triangles):

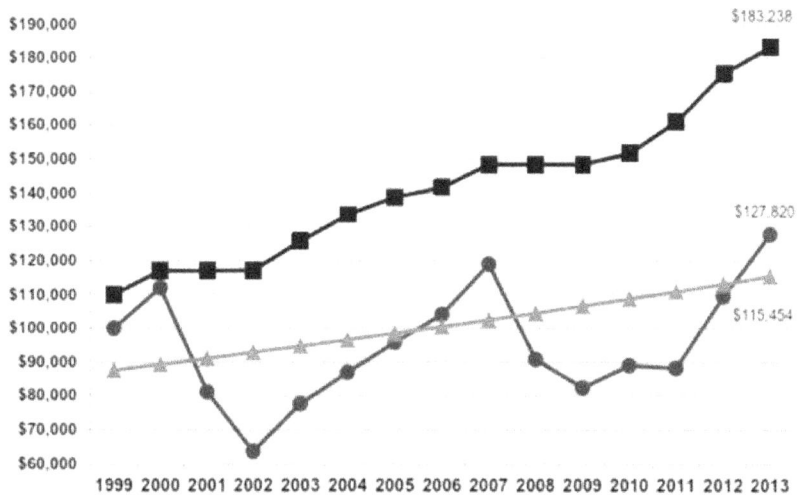

This graph is a hypothetical example using documented, historical S&P closing data.

You'll notice that even though the annuity was designed to mimic the performance of the S&P 500, in 2002 and 2009, when the index was falling, the annuity was still growing at the minimum guaranteed rate—protecting the annuitant from the downside risk in the market.

What's the Catch?

Annuities aren't for everyone. You should go through a financial review to discover the amount of money that's suitable for you to put into an annuity. You also have a lot of options to explore. You can get anything from a one-year annuity to a sixteen-year annuity. The one you pick should fit you particular situation and timeline.

Due to surrender periods, you'll want to make sure the money you put into an annuity won't need to be liquid and that you are viewing the arrangement as a long-term contract.

Chapter 9

Achieving Your Retirement Dreams

The last thing anyone should have to worry about when they retire is money. You've spent your whole life concerned about money—your retirement years are the time to harvest all that effort and sacrifice, and invest in more than just stocks or bonds—invest in yourself and your family.

The least you should be able to secure for yourself during these nonworking years is a living wage that keeps you feeling safe and secure and prevents you from sacrificing your standard of living. At this point, in order to gain such security and hold onto it, it's vital that you shift from a thought process of accumulation and risk into one of preservation and guarantees. At this point, you're either winding down the working years or you're entering the distribution phase. Accumulation isn't the priority now. Preservation, holding onto everything you have accumulated, is. Without holding onto what you've got, there will be nothing to distribute in the future.

Your past financial successes and gains are only as good as the income they provide to you in retirement. Thankfully, they don't have to work alone to secure your future and ensure your postretirement income. By designing the right postretirement financial plan, you can choose investments and contracts that take some of the pressure off you and your money while adding some safety nets to your future income.

The goal of every pre- and postretiree is to get the most out of their retirement savings. That can mean different things to different people. To some, it means creating a lifetime of income that can support and allow them to enjoy their retirement years in the way they have looked forward to. For others, it means growing their savings and taking out lump-sum withdrawals when need be, with the option of eventually starting a regular income withdrawal. For still others, it means having an emergency means of retirement funds but also creating a legacy for their heirs. And for still others, it means a combination of these things.

No matter what your retirement dreams are, an indexed annuity alone (or one with a death benefit and/or guaranteed income rider) can get you there without many of the constraints that a retirement account and traditional retirement investments impose and with guarantees that keep you safe throughout your retirement.

Chapter 10

Advisor Compensation

On a final note, one of my biggest pet peeves is the topic of compensation for agents and advisors. It's never a pleasant topic to discuss. From an objective standpoint, an advisor has worked for decades to develop an expertise that he shares with his clients. For that, compensation is not only necessary but also deserved and completely earned.

But I've been in the business a long time and I've watched as the concept of compensation has been used against advisors providing a valuable service to clients. I've also seen how it's been twisted into a weapon between specialists. I see how competitors go back and forth throwing jabs to one-up each other. I have seen blatant ads in newspapers and on websites—complete articles that focus only on why an investor should deal with advisors paid a certain way, and then the very next day, an article in the same location about why investors *shouldn't* deal with advisors paid that way. It's a never-ending, back-and-forth struggle, and while the target in the argumentative crosshairs may be advisors, the real victims are the investors who don't know what kind of advisor to choose or who to trust.

If we think back to that quote by Loren Dutton in Chapter 2, discussing the goal and purpose of financial planners, we quickly realize that this is not about competition, higher earnings and one-upmanship; our job is to help those who aren't in the financial industry, and who maybe don't understand it very well, to have the same chance at a comfortable retirement and financial future as everyone else. Brokers and advisors, like me, are here to level the playing field to help you achieve and maintain financial independence. That's not a competition—it's a duty.

I'd like to take this opportunity to clear the air and maybe relieve some pressure from those of you who aren't sure how to choose an advisor. The reality is, there is no right or wrong way for an advisor to get paid because there are so many different ways for the planning and the payment to happen.

Industry Stresses

When you meet with your financial advisor to talk about your goals and design an investment plan that meets them, you see a put-together individual who really knows his or her stuff. But there's a lot going on behind the scenes that helps get your advisor to that point.

For every hour your advisor spends with you discussing investment and planning options and educating you about all the different choices you have, there are several hours spent back in his or her office studying the industry, regulation changes, new investments and industries and so on.

And it's not all self-study, although that takes a good bit of your advisor's behind-the-scenes time. It's also about the various classes and courses and study he or she must do in order to meet regulated continuing education requirements, obtain licenses and achieve designations.

A good advisor invests much more of him- or herself than you will ever see. But you reap the rewards when you find an advisor who knows the industry inside and out, who takes the time necessary to comply with regulations, and who considers your needs, goals and risk tolerance when helping you make financial decisions.

No Advisor Works for Free

There are many ways that an advisor can get paid. Some are fee-based, meaning they charge a flat hourly fee that you pay, whether you take the advisor's advice or not. Others receive commissions on the products you buy or sell. Some may charge a set management fee. Still others receive a one-time commission on a life or annuity contract you enter into.

One thing I can promise you: not a single advisor you meet with is working for free. Whether it's a securities rep receiving an annual fee to manage your money, an advisor who sells a product and is paid directly from a company—which means that the payment itself does not come out of any of your funds nor does it hinder the growth of your funds—or it's a paid planner who doesn't execute the steps you decide to take but rather helps you decide what moves will be best to ensure your financial future, each one of these individuals is going to somehow receive payment for their time and services.

In mutual funds, there is something called a no-load fund. These are funds that have no commission fee (or load) when bought or sold, which is generally a very good deal for investors. But this lack of a front- or back-end load doesn't make them free of charge. Even in no-load funds, there can be an extremely aggressive expense ratio that is charged, sometimes daily, against the amount of the fund that you own. In addition, if the no-load funds are purchased and held within a brokerage or retirement account with an annual fee that you must pay to the brokerage firm holding the account, then you are making a payment in order to have the funds.

Even someone working at the bank is getting paid hourly to open your CD account. The point is, no matter where you go or what type of representative you talk to or receive financial advice from, they will at some point get paid.

It's not worth it to get hung up on the whys and hows of the payment made to your advisor or broker. In many ways, you've got no dog in that fight. Instead, it's better to educate yourself about finances in general. Understanding how the market works, how risky certain stocks are, the differences between various investments and so on will not only empower you on a general basis, it will also help you see through an advisor who is working to beef up his or her own commissions at the expense of your financial security.

With knowledge about the industry, you can ensure that you only deal with an advisor who is aligning your goals and values with his or her advice, and who is looking out for you and your family's best interests at all times—in other words, an advisor who's servicing your portfolio the way he or she should.

Additional Resources

[1] Ernst & Young LLP, July 2008, **Retirement vulnerability of new retirees: the likelihood of outliving their assets,** http://www.paycheckforlife.org

[2] Bureau of Labor Statistics, January 2013, **Consumer Price Index Summary,** http://www.bls.gov/news.release/cpi.nr0.htm

[3] Bureau of Labor Statistics, January 2013, **U.S. city averages all items,** ftp://ftp.bls.gov/pub/special.requests/cpi/cpiai.txt

[4] The Commonwealth Fund, August 2009, **New Report: Employer-Sponsored Health Insurance Premiums Increase 119 Percent from 1999-2008; Projected to Double Again by 2020,** http://www.commonwealthfund.org/News/News-Releases/2009/Aug/Employer-Sponsored-Health-Insurance-Premiums-Increase-119-Percent.aspx

[5] Fidelity.com, May 2012, **Fidelity® Estimates Couples Retiring in 2012 Will Need $240,000 to Pay Medical Expenses Throughout Retirement,**

http://www.fidelity.com/inside-fidelity/individual-
investing/retiree-health-care-costs-2012

[6] Social Security Administration, January 2009, **What young workers should know about Social Security and saving**

[7] BlackStar Funds, Accessed January 2013, **The Capitalism Distribution**, http://thecapitalismdistribution.pdf

[8] Highbeam Business, 2013, **Security Brokers, Dealers and Flotation Companies SIC 6211**,
http://business.highbeam.com/industry-
reports/finance/security-brokers-dealers-flotation-companies

[9] Wharton Financial Institutions Center Personal Finance, December 2010, **Real World Index Annuity Returns**,
http://fic.wharton.upenn.edu/fic/Policy%20page/RealWorld
Returns-revisedDec2010.pdf

[10] *USA TODAY*, November 9, 2011, **Money fund yields in variable annuities often less than zero,**
http://www.usatoday.com/money/perfi/funds/story/2011-11-
09/losing-money-in-a-money-fund/51143222/1

[11] National Organization of Life & Health Insurance Guaranty Associations, 2010, **Impairments & Insolvencies,** http://www.nolhga.com/factsandfigures/main.cfm/location/insolvencies

[12] Federal Deposit Insurance Corporation, March 9, 2012, **Failed Bank List,**

http://www.fdic.gov/bank/individual/failed/banklist.html

DESIGNING YOUR LIFE

What would happen if you discovered you could do more than just live your life—you could *design* it? This book teaches you to harness the power of your subconscious and program it to help you live a happy life fitting your definition of perfection.

DESIGNING YOUR LIFE: ACTION GUIDE

These exercises help you master your subconscious, abolish negativity and raise self-esteem. This guide focuses on creative visualization and powerful affirmations, to control your life's design and master your future.

DEVELOPING PERSEVERANCE

A combination of internal roadblocks are holding you back, preventing you from persevering. This book shows you how to break through these self-imposed obstacles to begin moving along your true path, taking you further than you ever thought possible.

DEVELOPING PERSEVERANCE: ACTION GUIDE

With this guide, you'll learn about the unique roadblocks you've designed for yourself and explore the thoughts, feelings and events that impact your ability to succeed.

YOU DESERVE TO BE RICH

If you're busy blaming your lack of wealth on upbringing, education and environment, you're missing out on learning how easy it is to get rich. This book teaches you to throw away the excuses and focus on the 12 steps to securing a future of financial success.

YOU DESERVE TO BE RICH: ACTION GUIDE

You deserve an ideal life. This workbook helps you get there by providing activities and strategies that explain the rules of greatness, help define your dreams and work to banish your fears.

UNLEASH YOUR MOJO

You already possess everything you need to be the person you want to be, you just have to access these powerful traits. In *Unleash Your Mojo*, you'll learn to recognize all the greatness inside you and discover how to put it to use and start living your ideal life.

UNLEASH YOUR MOJO: ACTION GUIDE

Each of us has power to succeed yet many of us never tap into that power. Instead we stagnate on the sidelines while others flash forward in life. This workbook gives practical tips, advice and exercises to advance in your quest for authenticity and power.

THE POSITIVE EDGE

There's a secret behind living a happy, successful, fulfilling life: *Positivity*. Learn how to overcome your tendency toward negativity, how to control your life and future, and how easy it is to improve your confidence and self-esteem.

SPARK: THE KEY TO IGNITING RADICAL CHANGE IN YOUR BUSINESS

A complete, step-by-step training program to help you become a high performer and higher earner. Learn how to rise to the top of your profession, position yourself as an expert and attract the abundance you desire.

DARE TO SUCCEED

Get the motivation and the information you need to rise to the next level of success! America's #1 Success Coach, Jack Canfield, has gathered together the top business minds in one powerful book. This guide contains their secret strategies to conquer the competition and bring ongoing abundance into your life.

VICTORY JOURNAL

The *Victory Journal* demonstrates the importance of writing down all your daily wins. Inside you'll find exercises to help define your ideal self and create action steps to move closer to your goals.

HARNESSING THE POWER OF GRATITUDE

Recognize the positive energy moving through your day and harness it with this undated journal. Filled with inspirational quotes to help you maintain the spirit of gratitude, it's an ideal tool for developing an enduring, powerful habit of thankfulness.

APPRECIATING ALL THAT YOU HAVE

This 365-day journal filled with inspirational quotes provides a safe space to write down the many things you're thankful for. It's the perfect way to help shift your perspective and recognize the abundance of positive forces in your life.

THE PSYCHOLOGY OF SALES:
FROM AVERAGE TO RAINMAKER

Take your sales from lackluster to rainmaker without any smarm, aggressive tactics or dishonesty. This book teaches sales pros the psychology of their customers so they can present products the right way for each shopper.

THE PSYCHOLOGY OF SALES: ACTION GUIDE

In this action guide, you'll gain greater insight into your own personality and psychological makeup as well as that of your customers so you can further your sales success and transform your career.

RETIREMENT YOU CAN'T OUTLIVE

Cut through the hype and challenge conventional wisdom with a book focusing on conservative and reasonable ways to save for retirement. This book uses plain language and lots of common sense that's been missing from financial planning sessions for decades.

RETIREMENT YOU CAN'T OUTLIVE: ACTION GUIDE

Transform the lessons taught in *Retirement You Can't Outlive* into action steps that change the shape of your financial future. This immersive tool contains worksheets, exercises and review sheets to help you develop a plan to rescue your financial future.

NAVIGATING THROUGH MEDICARE

Don't be confused by the rules, plans and parts of Medicare. This book simplifies the complex system and allows you to quickly and easily make the right decision for the future of your healthcare. It's a one-stop guide to everything you need to know.

AVOIDING A LEGACY NIGHTMARE

Poor planning can rip your estate from your loved ones. *Avoiding a Legacy Nightmare* is a simple guide to help you get started in creating an effective estate plan that achieves all that you intended.

PHYSICIANS: MONEY FOR LIFE

If you want to retire on your own terms, you must understand the special considerations that physicians need to make in order to maintain sustainable retirement plans. *Physicians: Money for Life* casts aside traditional advice that's not suited to conservative retirement planning and focuses on helping physicians design a plan that creates money for life.

PHYSICIANS: MONEY FOR LIFE: ACTION GUIDE

You have the knowledge necessary to change the financial health of your retirement, now it's time to apply it. This action guide helps you transform the lessons taught in *Physicians: Money for Life* into action steps you can take to change the shape of your retirement. With worksheets, exercises and review, this guide will help you move forward in your retirement planning journey while devising a plan to save it.

ALZHEIMER'S LEGACY GUIDE

Alzheimer's patients and their caregivers face a race against the clock and must learn how to cement a well-thought-out legacy plan before the disease's mental, emotional and psychological effects start to take their toll. This book provides guidance to both the recently diagnosed and those who will care for them as the disease progresses.

FINANCING YOUR LIFE: THE STORY OF FOUR FAMILIES

This is the story of four families that took their financial lives out of the red and into the black. There's McKenna, a single mom of two boys, working hard every day as a waitress; Toby and Shannon, two professionals battling a layoff and personal spending demons; Blake and Christine, a newlywed couple in a hurry to start living the good life, whether they can afford it or not; and Marcie and Kurt, two young parents struggling to keep up in an increasingly image-obsessed society.

FINANCING YOUR LIFE: THE FINANCIAL RECOVERY KIT

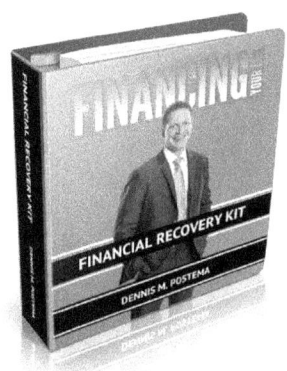

Financing Your Life is an innovative financial recovery kit devoted to teaching you how to take total control over your financial life. Within, you'll learn about the secret behind financial planning, budgeting basics, insurance, credit repair, getting out of debt, developing financial compromise with a spouse or partner, saving and investing, mortgages and more. This tool does more than just tell you about financial concepts; it helps you begin immediately integrating what you learn into your own financial life.

www.ingramcontent.com/pod-product-compliance
Lightning Source LLC
Chambersburg PA
CBHW051704170526
45167CB00002B/533